Alternative Futures and the
History of Political Thought

A BRIEF HISTORY *of*

POLITICAL THOUGHT

and STATECRAFT

FROM SOCRATES TO ROUSSEAU

HEGEL AND MARX

TOMORROW'S WORLD OF FREE NATIONS

THE POLITICAL THOUGHT OF G.W.F. HEGEL

*With an Introduction
and Illustrations*

HENRY PAOLUCCI

Preface by ANNE PAOLUCCI
Foreword by JACK RYAN

Copyright @ 2004 by Anne Paolucci

Library of Congress Cataloging-in-Publication Data

Paolucci, Henry.
 A brief history of political thought and statecraft :
Alternative futures and the history of political thought / by
Henry Paolucci.
  p. cm.
Three lectures based on three courses offered in the
Graduate Division of the Dept. of Government and Politics at
St. John's U. in New York. In 1978, they were adapted for
three CBS TV talks introducing a nationally televised series
titled 'Alternative futures.'
 ISBN 1-932107-08-8 (alk. Paper)
 1. Political science—History. 2. Political science—Philosophy.
I. Title: Alternative futures and the history of political thought.
II. Title.
 JA81.P29 2003
 320.1'09—dc22

                                                2003056838

Published for
THE BAGEHOT COUNCIL
by
GRIFFON HOUSE PUBLICATIONS
P. O. BOX 468
SMYRNA, DE, 19977

CONTENTS

LIST OF ILLUSTRATIONS

PREFACE

First published in 1979, this brief but wide-sweeping account of major political thinkers and statesmen, from Aristotle to Abba Eban, and of the historical realities they helped shape, remains a tour-de force. The author's command of sources and his rigorous commitment to the facts of history make this survey of political thought and practice, covering almost twenty-five centuries, a particularly valuable one.

Highlighting those thinkers and statesmen who left a major impact on the realities of political thought and life, Paolucci introduces us, with uncommon confidence and ease, to the awe-inspiring experience of the independent city-states of ancient Greece and the first efforts toward that individual freedom which finally became possible in the modern world. He guides us through the hard reality of the Roman experiment with world government and impresses upon us the tremendous impact of Machiavellian realpolitik on the evolution of modern states. In the chapter on "Hegel and Marx" he provides a brilliant juxtaposition of Hegel's view of history as an organic continuum and Karl Marx's insistence on the unhistorical absolute that all existing political structures, as creations of the past, must be destroyed. Finally, he brings our attention to focus on the tumultuous events of the last century, including two world wars, and anticipates the widespread threat of terrorism.

Hegel certainly was one of the most important influences in Henry Paolucci's intellectual life — a life that held together in an organic and integral whole much else, as well, and with the same regard for truth and intellectual honesty. His students especially remember him — even at a distance of over thirty years — as someone who never trimmed an argument, never discouraged Socratic exchange, and always gave the best possible account not only of authors he treasured but also of those with whom he did not agree.

In presenting the Hegelian view, both in the classroom and in his writings, he was accurate and clear; but he always, also, did justice to others, like Marx, explaining his revolutionary ideas, for example, in an exciting context worthy of their profound historical impact.

For the present edition, a fourth chapter has been added on the political thought of Hegel (originally published in 1978 as a 40 page monograph).* In it, Professor Paolucci gives us — here too, in a brief but substantial discussion — a more detailed account of Hegel's political philosophy.

ANNE PAOLUCCI
New York
September 5, 2003

——————————

(*Other articles, essays and books by Henry Paolucci on Hegel and his influence include *Hegel on the Arts* (Frederick Ungar; Griffon House Publications); *Hegel on Tragedy*, with Anne Paolucci (Doubleday Co., Harper & Row, Greenwood, GHP); "Hegel and the Celestial Mechanics of Newton and Einstein," in *Henry Paolucci: Selected Writings* (GHP); "Truth in the Philosophical Sciences of Society, Politics, and History," in *Beyond Epistomology* (Martinus Mijhoff) and *Henry Paolucci: Selected Writings* (GHP); "The Poetics of Aristotle and Hegel," in *Review of National Literatures* (Council on National Literatures); "Hegel and the Idea of Artistic Beauty or the Ideal," in *Henry Paolucci: Selected Writings* (GHP). Even this brief list is impressive testimony to Paolucci's commitment to the pursuit of knowledge and to the broad spectrum of his interests.)

FOREWORD

For all those who have a vital interest in the theories and methods by which nations are formed, this small volume is a treasure-trove of informative data and provocative discussion. Professor Paolucci has been brief and concise in covering every major aspect of nation-building over the last three millenia. His work ranks him high among the very statesmen, philosophers, and academics whose ideas he discusses in this book: Socrates and Plato in ancient Greece, Augustus Caesar and Polybius in the Roman era, St. Augustine in the Middle Ages, St. Thomas Aquinas, Dante and Thomas Cromwell in the Renaissance, Hobbes, Locke, and Rousseau in the years of the Reformation, to name the most conspicuous.

He takes particular interest in G. W. F. Hegel, many of whose writings he has translated and interpreted in various books and articles over the years. Another favorite of his was Walter Bagehot (whom he calls England's "Spare Chancellor," and after whom he launched, in 1967, The Walter Bagehot Research Council on National Sovereignty — still active today). He saw in Hegel the answer to Marx's classless and stateless society; and agreed with Bagehot that individual freedom is best insured by the presidential or parliamentary form of "government by discussion."

This work, though written some years ago, is especially timely as new nations are being structured in Africa and the Middle East. Our leaders, who are working in Iraq to help a diverse population form a lasting government, would do well to read Professor Paolucci on the subject.

JACK RYAN
The Bagehot Council

INTRODUCTION

The chapters of this book reproduce the texts of three lectures that sum up the substance of three courses offered in the Graduate Division of the Department of Government and Politics at St. John's University in New York. In 1978, they were adapted for three CBS TV talks introducing a nationally televised series titled "Alternative Futures." Printed versions had previously been issued to supplement assigned readings for courses described as follows:

(1) "*Great Political Thinkers: Ancient and Medieval.* The origins and development of political theory and statecraft in the writings of Plato, Aristotle, Polybius, St. Augustine, and St. Thomas, studied in the context of the historical experience of the ancient Athenians and Spartans, the Republican and Imperial Romans, the Ancient Jews and Early Christians, and the new Germanic peoples of the West down to the time of Dante."

(2) "*Great Political Thinkers: Modern.* A study of the political thought and statecraft of Machiavelli, Luther and Calvin, Hobbes, Spinoza, Locke, Montesquieu, Rousseau, Burke, Beccaria, Bentham and Mill, the American Federalists, Hegel, Tocqueville, Marx, Bagehot, Spencer, Maitland, and the revolutionary elitists and welfare-statists of the twentieth century."

(3) "*The Political Thought of Hegel and Marx.* A study of the major political writings of Hegel and Marx, emphasizing the systematic character of the former and the revolutionary force of the latter."

As delivered on the CBS TV series, the lectures were titled: (1) "Great Political Thinkers: Ancient, Medi-

1

eval, and Modern"; (2) "Hegel and Marx"; and (3) "Great Modern Political Thinkers and the Global Challenges of the Present."

For the version of the first lecture that makes up Chapter I of this *Brief History of Political Thought and Statecraft*, the author takes as his point of departure Aristotle's striking contrast of the political characters of the Asian, Greek, and West European peoples of antiquity, which serves even now to clarify the diverse attitudes toward the future that prevail in the East and the West and the lands in between. Guided by that Aristotelian insight, the author then traces the influence of Greek political thought first on the Romans, in their efforts to legislate for the world, and then on the mission of the Christian Church to educate the Germanic conquerors of Rome — a mission that culminates in the grand medieval design to balance and harmonize the ends and means of Christian grace with those of the classical value-system of nature. That balance is broken in the periods of the Renaissance and Reformation. And it is only then that the distinctive political task of the Western peoples, as contrasted with the ancient Greco-Roman and Asian peoples, finally emerges. Thereafter, the history of Western political thought and statecraft becomes the history of efforts to frame institutions of government that make possible not simply the rule of a single despot over great masses of virtually enslaved subjects, as in the ancient East; or the rule of oligarchies and democratic majorities based on the maintenance of a large service-class of slaves, as in the Greek city-states and Republican Rome; but rather the self-rule of adult peers aspiring to individual equality in freedom as citizens of a nationally-constituted political community, without the supporting services of slaves.

It was Machiavelli, in the chaotically-divided Italy of the early sixteenth century, who gave modern political thought its pessimistic experimental start. But for an account of the full extrication of Western statecraft from the tutelage of the medieval Church, the line one needs to pursue is that which leads from Machiavelli's English disciples Thomas Cromwell and Sir Francis Bacon, through Hobbes, Locke, Montesquieu, and Rousseau, to the French Revolution.

That world-historic French Revolution followed quickly on the heels of the American Revolution, but with an altogether different motivation. It was supposed to have inaugurated a perpetual reign of reason, enabling mankind to experiment freely and omnipotently, in an equality of brotherhood, with its own future. What it inaugurated instead was a reign of terror. And that terror, in turn, served to make the Western peoples historically self-conscious for the first time. The leading thinkers of the West came to recognize that the French Revolution's reign of terror was history's response to the presumption of the rationalist philosophers of the eighteenth century who had imagined they could uproot themselves from the past, and pull down all the institutions that have developed out of the past, on the strength of abstract reason alone. With the terror and its immediate consequences, history was demanding its due.

The significance for political thought and statecraft of the awakening of the historical sense in nineteenth-century Europe is the theme of the second chapter of this book. Having been shocked by the events of the French Revolution and of Napoleon's efforts to export its results, a new generation of Western thinkers came to recognize that history, including the history of particular peoples, has an inherent reason of its own, far more powerful than the anti-historical, abstract reasoning of rationalist philosophers. Without ceasing to be what they had been since the Renaissance and Reformation, without changing their basic characters, the Western peoples nevertheless recast completely their old views of themselves. It is in the writings of Hegel on ethics, law, economics, politics, history, art, religion, and philosophy that the new self-consciousness of the Western peoples is brought into comprehensive focus; and it is in the writings of Karl Marx on capitalism and class struggle that the revolutionary implications of the new attitude, viewed from an alien vantage-point, are given a most powerful, though one-sided expression.

The third chapter, titled "Tomorrow's World of Free Nations," takes up the contemporary implications of the awakening of the historical sense that dominated the development of political thought and statecraft down through the middle of the nineteenth century. By that time, as a consequence of what Hegel and Marx called the dialectic of capitalist-industrial expansion, the Western nations had attained a measure of global influence without precedent in human history. Marx and his revolutionary disciples, following the lead of the major English political-economists since the time of Adam Smith, had examined the "facts" of capitalist-industrial expansion as if they had nothing to do with national character and national political development. But other, less alien-minded contemporaries of Marx — like Walter Bagehot, for instance — saw clearly that the sudden burgeoning of economic productivity, in England and France particularly, was part of the same dynamic re-animating process, rooted in historical self-consciousness, that was revealing another aspect of its productive power in the labors of mid-nineteenth century statesmen like Bismarck, Cavour, and Lincoln to perfect the national unity of their peoples. Bagehot's provocative insights on this theme are reviewed in the third chapter, with special emphasis on his study of the future prospects of the four chief types of government under which most of the peoples of the world then seemed destined to live: the Parliamentary and the Presidential forms, based on public discussion and choice; and the Hereditary and the Dictatorial or Revolutionary forms, based on hardened custom, at one extreme, and the force of despotic expediency, at the other.

But the striking aspect of the development of Western political experience since the mid-nineteenth century has been its virtually immediate global impact. The result has been a quite obvious Westernization of the entire world. Whether it has arrived on the scene under positive auspices, like that of the traditional "promise of American life," or with the culturally-nihilistic force of Marxism, the Western inner experience of awakened national self-awareness is now affecting the aspirations for the future of all peoples everywhere — in the new and emergent as well as in the established and older neglected nations which together make up the world's rich diversity.

I. FROM SOCRATES TO ROUSSEAU

We begin this discussion on alternative futures with a backward look at some of the alternatives that the great political thinkers of the past have contemplated. Our capacity to look ahead is activated by self-consciousness. And that means looking back upon one's past. Awareness of one's national, cultural, religious roots provides the directive force for looking ahead.

It is awe-inspiring to realize that all the great civilizations of ancient times became self-consciously aware of their origins in this sense at approximately the same time: during the sixth century B.C. In a vast sweep, from East to West, that century gave us the enlightenment of Confucius in China, of Buddha in India, of Zoroaster in Mesopotamia, of the prophets Jeremiah and Ezekiel among the Jews of the Babylonian domination, and of Thales at the head of a host of speculative thinkers in Greece.

The commandment of enlightenment is in every instance the same: Know-Thyself. But for each people experiencing it, what comes to be known is of course its own cultural distinctiveness. Enlightenment in ancient China reveals an enduring identity of humanistic, disciplined, infinitely-detailed concern for the proprieties of conduct in family, clan, and civic relationships. In Buddha's India, it mirrors a self-consuming spirituality that is kept from annihilating all social relationships only by an inflexible caste system. In the Middle East, under the tolerant rule of the Persians, enlightenment mirrors the diverse characters of the Egyptians longing for a material continuance of life beyond the grave; of Assyrians anxious to enjoy the day's pleasures before night falls; and of faithful Jews awaiting a

Messiah yet fearing that he might already have come and gone unnoticed.

Greek Wisdom, Roman Power

In Greece, enlightenment can be said to start with Thales, but it is not concentrated in him. Just as Greek political life was fragmented into many city-states, so its enlightenment was quickly refracted into a thousand colors. And we quickly get the spectrum of one Greek mind after another affirming for itself the characteristically Greek conviction that a life lived *uncritically* — an *unexamined life* — is not worth living. Raphael has pictured the multiplicity of it in his celebrated Vatican painting of the leaders of Greek thought.

The *examined life,* the life constantly compared and contrasted with other lives to learn the truth about it — that is what we owe the Greeks, as a people, even now that they have long been gone. Contrasting the Greeks with his own nation, the Jews, St. Paul will say centuries later: "For the Jews require a sign and the Greeks seek after wisdom." By that he meant that the Jewish people want their lives to be ultimately determined by the commandments of divine revelation, whereas the Greeks always want rational explanations. The Greeks rationalized everything they touched with their thought. And it is that activity that gave rise to what we now call the science or rational study of politics. Plato was the poetic pioneer who provided infinitely suggestive myths about everything. He, as well as Aristotle, who summed up the political experience of the Greeks for us, was fully aware that there were other types of people, to the East and to the West of Greece, who had very different attitudes, and whose governments were, and ought to be, different. Aristotle, for instance, says at one point in his *Politics* that people in the Western and Northern parts of Europe are generally very spirited, even stubbornly individualistic in character, but not very intelligent or skillful as compared with the Greeks; and that is why they have never been capable of organizing themselves politically or of governing others. Asiatics, on the other hand, are for the most part intelligent and skillful, but lacking in spirit, and so, says Aristotle, they are "in continuous subjugation and slavery."

The Greeks, he then says, occupy a middle ground both geographically and temperamentally. They are both spirited and intelligent. They can organize themselves, but refuse to do so in large units. All they have ever wanted are political units no larger than suffices to make a critically-examined life possible.

For this reason, though he was the teacher of a would-be world ruler — Alexander the Great — Aristotle opposed the idea of world government. Each people should have its own form of government, he taught; for what might please the nations of the East might prove oppressive to the individualistic people of the northwest and restrictive for the Greek nation which could bring itself into some sort of unity only temporarily, for defense against a common enemy.

The trouble with the beautifully independent life of the Greek city-states was that, in the end, more or less barbaric neighbors, first the Macedonians and then the Romans, proved to be too powerful for it. The Greeks had their revenge, however, for they conquered their conquerors culturally. The Romans went to school at the feet of the Greeks. Through the influence largely of one man, a Greek hostage named Polybius, the best Roman families learned to think like Greeks about government and politics. Polybius wrote, in Greek, a history of the Romans from their legendary origins down to his own time, when his pupil, the famous Roman general Scipio Africanus the Younger defeated Hannibal's Carthage and established Rome as the most powerful state in the world. In that history, Polybius gives the Romans a detailed analysis of their natural character and of their political constitution, all from a Greek point of view. And in the course of that analysis he supplies

"SCHOOL OF ATHENS"
(Raphael)

THE PARTHENON OF ATHENS

SOCRATES
(469-399 B.C.)

PLATO
(427-347 B.C.)

ARISTOTLE
(384-322 B.C.)

ALEXANDER THE GREAT
(356-323 B.C.)

MOSES
(13th Century B.C.)

them with simplified versions, adapted to the needs of their more Western character, of all that Socrates, Plato, and Aristotle had had to say about statecraft, the ends of government, and the strengths and weaknesses of the various possible kinds of political constitutions.

But it is important to stress that the Romans were not like the Greeks in character, any more than the Greeks were like the Jews. Socrates, the typical Greek who seeks after wisdom, is not to be confounded with Moses who brought the divine commandments, the divine signs of God's will, to the Jews. And neither is the typical Roman, Julius Caesar, to be confounded with either of the other two. As they matured, the Romans had only one irresistible passion; and that was to legislate for the world.

The Greek political ideal had been that of a government that makes men *think* better, about beauty, truth, and goodness. The Romans rejected that notion. The purpose of government, in their view, was simply to preserve, protect, and defend their commonwealth at all costs, leaving it to the individual to find his beauty, truth, and goodness under a global regime of rigorously enforced peace. The organizer of that peace, after a century and a half of internal struggle among the demagogues, establishment leaders, and generals of republican Rome, was Augustus Caesar. Based on principles of law suited to the needs of world government, the peace he established was destined to be maintained, with a gradual extension of the rights of citizenship to all peoples of the Mediterranean world, for centuries. And, in time, the chief beneficiaries of that Roman peace became so devoted to it that they ceased to be willing to fight at all, even to restrain terrorists in their midst or marauding bands on their borders.

Clever statesmen eventually worked up schemes to use terrorists to check terrorists, while the Romans themselves sank deeper and deeper into the habits of peace. But finally those terrorists came to believe they had learned enough to run the government they had been protecting for themselves. And so, in 410 A.D., the chief of the Goths in Northern Italy — Alaric — decided to sack the city of Rome. It had been exactly eight-hundred years since the Eternal City had suffered such a fate, and that had been in almost legendary primitive times when Rome had only a small population and ruled only itself. How could the imperial capital of the world permit itself to be sacked by terrorists who were, in effect, employees of the global peace-keeping establishment?

The Stumbling-block of Christ Crucified

But the really terrible thing about that sack of Alaric was that, just fifteen years earlier, in 395 A.D., the Roman imperial government had outlawed its traditional pagan religion, with its gods of fortune, peace, and war, to establish in its place, an oriental cult of peace known as Christianity. The founder of Christianity, Jesus of Nazareth, had let himself be crucified by Roman soldiers without fighting. In 395 A.D., after centuries of Roman persecution, his religion had become the religion of Rome itself. And so the few remaining pagan intellectuals of the empire could not resist crying out: Fifteen years of official Christianity, and see what happens! Rome is sacked for the first time in eight-hundred years!

Roman Christian intellectuals protested in turn, after the shock had worn off, that — except for the shock — it really had not been anything to get too disturbed about. Soon, they said, the barbarian peoples of Northern Europe would all be converted. One after another, they would all seek admittance into Rome's world-wide church and world-wide peace-keeping state. That was an alternative future, they insisted, well worth the price of a three-day sack of Rome, if only the pagan intellectuals, still dreaming of the old Roman virtues, could be brought to their senses.

Which was to be preferred: a pagan Roman or a Christian Roman world peace? That was the great debate of the chief varieties of one-worlders in the early fifth

JULIUS CAESAR
(102-44 B.C.)

AUGUSTUS CAESAR
(63 B.C.-14 A.D.)

"THE CRUCIFIXION"
(Antonello da Messina)

century A.D. Against both, a powerful voice was raised. It was the voice of the most important political thinker of Christendom, the learned North African saint and bishop, Augustine of Hippo Regius.

Augustine joins Aristotle, from an opposite direction, in condemning the idea of imposing enforceable world peace upon the world, especially when the force is to be applied in the name of Christ. To pursue such a peace seems noble; yet, really, for those empowered to enforce it, it means ultimately having their will with everyone, everywhere in the world. Christians are tempted by the idea because they like to think that God's peace, if ever it were realized on earth, would have to be global; so why not prepare for it by opposing a plurality of states, meanwhile, and favoring a one-world state?

Against that early notion of secular-Christian convergence on a new benignly peaceful variety of world-state, or global village, St. Augustine raised his voice and pen to warn that, Christians, at any rate, cannot in good faith constitute any sort of state of their own in this world (least of all one with an absolute monopoly of coercive peace-keeping power), because they cannot, in good faith, have a politics of their own. The only politics possible on earth, he admonishes, is that of coercive power used to restrain coercive power. That is why Christ said to Pilate that his kingdom was not of this world, that had it been of this world his followers would have fought to prevent his crucifixion. Christians who live like Christ — who tolerate Pilate's power — don't need temporal government for themselves. Temporal government is needed for those who don't live like Christ; for those who seek their own in the world and more than their own. Its global extension would therefore be essentially the extension of a vast prison in which rulers restrain everybody else but are not restrained themselves till corruption brings them down.

That is the last powerful voice of the Greco-Roman world before the northern European peoples, the ungovernable individualists that Aristotle spoke of, swarm in upon it. It is a Christian voice, but a very realistic pessimistic voice. It was raised at precisely the time when, after being pounded incessantly by the spirited violence of marauding bands at its borders, the Roman peace-keeping system literally collapsed and began withering away. Only the Roman Christian Church, armed with the wisdom of Augustine, survived to educate the new peoples, both religiously and politically.

Grace and Nature

The historical record shows that the genuinely political experience of the Western European peoples was acquired entirely within the Church from above, and that it took almost a thousand years of priestly education to prepare those spirited peoples for self-government from below. Only as late as the thirteenth century did St. Thomas Aquinas, with alternative futures in mind, begin to encourage the idea that political government should be regarded as human in character, not divine, as belonging to nature, not grace. Christian grace, he said, doesn't remove nature, it merely completes or *perfects* it.

Aristotle had said that all men by nature desire to know, desire to be happy, and desire the life of political community which is the *natural* means for attaining earthly knowledge and happiness. That is all to the good, said St. Thomas, provided only that it is not mistaken for the *highest* good. Pursue knowledge naturally, indeed; but don't push it so far that you lose Christian faith. And don't push the natural pursuit of happiness or of political community so far that you lose Christian hope and love in the process. One must remember that the love that nourishes Christian hope is love of one's enemies in war as well as of one's friends and fellow-citizens.

St. Thomas seemed to sense that bad times were coming for a Christendom whose rulers, despite St. Augustine's teachings, were aspiring to rule the world as

ST. AUGUSTINE
(354-430 A.D.)

ST. THOMAS AQUINAS
(1225-1274)

DANTE ALIGHIERI
(1265-1321)

Christian, with an authority which came to them they claimed *not* from the Pope as Vicar of Christ, but directly from God, by divine right. St. Thomas said that, apart from the authority of grace, transmitted exclusively by the Church, rulers could have only natural authority, derived from God indeed, but only indirectly, through the consent of the people — whose voice, when they speak as "we the people," is the natural voice of God in politics. When the German Holy Roman Emperors — the Hohenstaufen emperors — insisted on the right of grace directly from God, the Papacy forced their overthrow, with the help of many professedly Christian kings and communes. But those kings and communes quickly claimed for themselves what the emperors had claimed, and the Church was then worse off in this respect than before.

That is what led the great Italiao poet, Dante Alighieri, author of *The Divine Comedy,* to make a final plea for restoration of a divine-right Christian empire of grace, to enforce world peace while the Church confined itself to administering the sacraments. Otherwise, Dante prophesied, Christians would sooner or later be split into powerful sects and warring nations, each claiming to have Christian grace on its side; and then the whole world would sink into a new paganism, without peace, without Church, and without God.

The balance that St. Thomas had hoped to maintain between grace and nature soon tipped almost wholly toward one side, the side of nature. We call the age in which this happened the Renaissance; and this was soon followed by another age, called the Reformation, which cuts up the unity of the Christian church into hundreds of pieces. But in between these two ages, Italy produces a political thinker of shocking originality who puts political thought on a new course from which it has never since removed itself. That man, whose name was destined to become synonymous with that of the devil — Niccolo Machiavelli — is of course the author of that notorious tract on experimental, scientific statecraft, titled *The Prince.*

Machiavelli in his day was very much concerned with alternative futures. Italy then consisted of many states: highly civilized communes, primarily, which were not, however, founded — like the Greek city-state — on slavery. The trouble with civilized multiplicity in Italy was that, as in ancient Greece, less civilized but united neighboring peoples had an incalculable advantage. In Machiavelli's day, Italy's French and more distant Spanish neighbors had in fact marched in and were behaving worse than Alaric's Goths.

What is to be done? That was Machiavelli's persistent question long before it became Lenin's. Italians, he replied, had somehow to be united politically for the common defense. Yet who at that time had enough respect as a leader to do it? The Pope, surely. But the Pope can't be induced to do it because he wants still to keep his Church global, supranational, in character and influence. So Christianity in its present universal form, Machiavelli concludes, must be discounted politically, at least with respect to Italy's immediate needs. What is needed, instead, is a leader who will not shrink from doing whatever has to be done to force the Italians to be one. Anticipating the advent of such a leader, Machiavelli writes a method-book on the subject. And his method is quite unmistakably that of the *experimental model.*

The idea of the experimental model, as applied in political thought and statecraft, is to search ancient and contemporary history for examples of political success or failure in comparable cases. And that is what Machiavelli does. In ancient Greece, in Rome, in France, in a neighboring Italian commune, such and such a thing was done, and this was the result. In a similar situation elsewhere, something else was done, and the result was different. By this means, Machiavelli begins to work up experimentally-valid laws of statecraft — laws which, he says, permit a statesman to turn knowledge into power.

Modern Statecraft and Modern Science

Machiavelli got the science of statecraft right. Everyone who reads him senses that. But the situation in Italy was too difficult, too complex — primarily, Machiavelli felt, because the Pope's presence prohibited effective use of Christianity for political purposes. But what couldn't be done in Italy soon became very possible elsewhere. Machiavellian experimental statecraft had its first serious application in England, because there things were not at all as divided as they were in Italy.

England's great Machiavellian was a younger contemporary named Thomas Cromwell, third of the three great Thomases who served under Henry VIII at the time of the Reformation. (The other two were Thomas Wolsey, who was ineffectual finally, and Thomas More, who was beheaded on orders from Cromwell, acting for his king.) Thomas Cromwell has gone down in history, like Machiavelli, as a great villain. But he is, in fact, the villain who, virtually alone, with his Machiavellian statecraft, made possible the glorious Elizabethan age of England that gave us Edmund Spenser, Shakespeare, and Sir Francis Bacon.

Thomas Cromwell did some terrible things to make England great, and he paid dearly for it, with his head. Nevertheless, he deserves to be ranked as England's greatest political thinker in the practical sense, as well as its greatest statesman. For he made possible the constitutional arrangements that English political thinkers have been discussing and analyzing and comparing and contrasting with other constitutions ever since — from Thomas Hobbes, James Harrington, and John Locke, through John Stuart Mill and Walter Bagehot, to Maitland, Harold Laski, and Michael Oakeshott.

Cromwell made possible a *continued* growth of the form of parliamentary-monarchic government — of government of the king *in* Parliament — that had ruled England since the end of the thirteenth century. This he achieved by inducing Henry VIII not only to separate himself from Rome — to make England fully free — but also to do it with the approval of Parliament and *in* Parliament. That Parliament was then a rubber-stamp institution. Henry could have done without its approval. But Cromwell, looking ahead to a time when kings could no longer claim divine right, made provision for the future. He saw to it that, if ever an English king had to give up divine right claims, a Parliament speaking for the people would be at hand with long-established precedents.

In practice, Cromwell's English statecraft was Machiavellian to the core. But a theoretic formulation of it was provided a little later by the celebrated Sir Francis Bacon, a contemporary of Shakespeare, a great prose writer, and also a high minister of state. He is, of course, universally honored as the founder of modern empirical and experimental science. He could not himself have been a practicing scientist in the strict sense, for he knew nothing of the scientific uses of higher mathematics. But he was most eloquent in calling upon the English government to finance and facilitate the advance of such science in the public interest.

Bacon advises his peers to turn to Machiavelli, who studied politics experimentally to teach princes how to gain power over other men. The trouble with poor Machiavelli, he explains, is that he had to work in disunited Italy and therefore had first to propose a way of destroying the centers of disunity before his method could be used to *build*. In unified England, his method could, on the contrary, be applied to strengthen the economic base of an already unified political community. And from that base, one could gradually work upward to rationalize the entire superstructure, to the very top.

Hobbes, Locke, and Rousseau

Sir Francis Bacon had a young assistant named Thomas Hobbes, upon whom he made a powerful impression.

NICCOLO MACHIAVELLI
(1469-1527)

THOMAS HOBBES
(1588-1679)

JOHN LOCKE
(1632-1704)

JEAN-JACQUES ROUSSEAU
(1712-1778)

Hobbes had a clear sense of the fact that Englishmen were not like those oriental peoples Aristotle spoke of who are so servile that they often let themselves be enslaved collectively. He had a clear sense also that Englishmen were not like the ancient Greeks, who were by and large free, but who nevertheless had enough servile people in their midst to build their civilization on slavery. Englishmen, Hobbes is convinced, never, never can be slaves; but that means they are apt to fight one another individualistically forever — once freed from the tutelage of the Church — unless they can work up enough intelligence to do something rational about it without becoming needlessly servile. What has to be done, says Hobbes, is simple: we — all of us — have to agree to concentrate the force of our spirited individualism in a single person or group that will thereafter exercise the force of individualism itself, to protect our individualism.

That is the Hobbesian legacy to the modern world: the idea of replacing a governmental order imposed from above by way of priests and kings schooled in the Greco-Roman-Hebraic tradition, with a new order organized from below, by and through the consent of the governed. The so-called social-contract theory serves here only as an experimental model. One way or another, all subsequent political thinkers in the West will work with experimental models of the social-contract type to test hypotheses and to gain the kind of knowledge about government and politics that can be converted into power. Hobbes in 1651 used the model, as we said, to show that, when free men are in a natural state of war of each against all, they need to agree to institute an absolute government if they are to be safe and free as individuals. Once that lesson was learned in England, John Locke used the model in 1690 to show that Englishmen could enjoy the rights of life, liberty, property without an absolute government, or any government at all, if they had a disposition to do so, and that they needed to agree only to establish a constitutional monarchy to be

secure and free *without inconveniences*. The American founding fathers took it a step further: after their revolution of
1776, they used it to show that individuals who love liberty
enough can certainly get on with governments like the one
recommended by Locke; but also that, where an ocean
intervenes, they can also do so without a king. From
Hobbes to Locke, to the American Federalists, indeed, the
model changes to the point where it can be said that the
individualism of free and equal men and women enables
them to rule themselves most satisfactorily on the principle
that the government that governs *least* governs *best*.

But what about France? In France, fullest use is
made of the social-contract model by Jean Jacques Rousseau
whose book on the subject — the revolutionary *Contract
Social* published in 1762 — is world famous. Rousseau
rejects the idea that, in the state of nature, apart from civil
society, free men and women would behave like wild
beasts. He agrees, instead, with his fellow Frenchman, the
learned Baron de Montesquieu, that isolated human beings, each acting alone, don't really represent much of a
danger to one another. Surely what divided Italy, in Machiavelli's day, for instance, was not individuals acting alone,
but organized groups fighting organized groups.

That, according to Rousseau, was obviously what
plagued France. In France, he argued, the intermediary
groups, especially the great noble feudal houses, had in
fact prevented France from ever being united the way
England was after 1066, and again under Henry VIII. The
feudal heritage that could be preserved with unity in
England, he thought, would therefore have to be destroyed
in France if there was ever to be true unity of government.
Accordingly, with his social-contract model, Rousseau urges
that every intermediate group in France be broken up,
leaving every individual to act on his own, freely and
equally. First of all the old monarchy and the old Church
would have to be destroyed. Why not gain unity by uniting
church and state in one head, as the English King and the

Russian Czar have done? That won't do, says Rousseau, because it merely brings the opposition of temporal and religious values into the very heart of government itself. No, the solution is to have only one group in politics — the group of the whole — and nothing but isolated, free individuals, equal in their freedom and isolation, at the opposite extreme.

From that we get the motto of the French Revolution. With the slate of the past cleared of all prior organizations, there will now be the purest sort of Liberty, and of course Equality for *all* in Liberty. But then, on what basis will these free and equal individualists draw together to form a more perfect union than they ever enjoyed before? Rousseau's answer is that the very desire, shared by all, to be free and equal, will unite them as brothers. And that provides the third term of the motto: Liberty, Equality, and Fraternity.

Rousseau suggests that such a feeling could unite mankind. Still, the important thing, first, is to wipe the slate clean, obliterate the old order in its entirety. The French Revolution of 1789 attempted to do just that, in a phase of rational destruction carried through on the basis of the experimental model of the social contract. A constructive phase was, of course, to start immediately thereafter. The end product would be an alternative future organized as a reign of reason, cleansed of all the ignorance, all the error, all the injustice of the past. An English poet who visited Paris in the days of the inauguration of this reign of reason, cried out:

Great was it in that dawn to be alive
But to be young was very heaven.

And so it was. Very soon, however, as we all know, that reign of reason became a reign of terror. Reason claimed to have triumphed over history; but history quickly had its revenge. You don't uproot your past as easily as that!

History quickly taught the heads of the French Revolution and their admirers abroad that history has its own reason, its own rationality. It is reason *in* history, not reason *against* history that is powerful. Things like the French Revolution don't come about without historical preparation. And history often makes such things happen for reasons far removed from anything that the revolutionary agitators may have had in mind or even dreamt of.

But this new appreciation of the power of history itself to determine alternative futures is the theme of Part II: on the historical-minded philosopher Hegel, author of a great *Philosophy of History*, and on the historically-minded revolutionary, Karl Marx, author, with Friedrich Engels, of *The Communist Manifesto*.

II. HEGEL AND MARX

From the time of Machiavelli to the start of the French Revolution, political thought in the West tended to become steadily more optimistic about man's capacity to control his future. There was a gradually strengthened conviction that human intelligence, if methodically applied, could master the forces of nature to satisfy all the material needs of men, now and in the future. But, as we noted in the last chapter, the beginnings in Machiavelli's time were dark. Renaissance Italy was then being devastated by foreign armies, and Christendom's once-seamless garment of faith was being torn to shreds by the Reformation. In fact, it was something very close to despair that prompted men like Machiavelli to roll up their sleeves and attempt something new, something experimental.

What I am saying is that it is a mistake to think of the start of the modern world, with the birth of experimental science, as a happy time. Representational art can help us here; for a great sad artist living in the time of Machiavelli, Luther, and Thomas Cromwell, has expressed for us in masterful design what the impulse that gave birth to modern science was really all about. The artist's name is Albrecht Dürer, and the date of his representation is about 1520. It is a stupendous, bronze colossus of a winged woman, seated on a kind of throne. She leans forward massively, clasping an open book on her lap. In her right hand she holds a pair of compasses, and scattered about her feet are all sorts of instruments of science. A comet hangs in the heavens, with a massive rainbow, anything but cheerful, arched in front of it. And beyond the steeples of a distant village, held aloft by a kind of bat, is the name that explains it all: *Melencolia* — interpreted here as the power of hopelessness, the strength of despair, of lost hope that creates from its own wreck the thing it contemplates.

This winged superhuman woman, this spirit of science, stares with eyes full set into the future. What does she see? Perhaps a vision of that great distant day when science will make a show of its ultimate triumph over the powers of nature, by turning this dull earth first into a miniature blazing star, then quickly into a mushrooming smoky mass, and finally into a burned-out ash.

Shakespeare expressed that kind of despair in *Macbeth* and in *Hamlet.* And Sir Francis Bacon too felt it powerfully, even while he was formulating policy to harness its strength for the commonwealth. Bacon was the Energy Czar of his day. His new and comprehensive energy plan, called the *Great Instauration,* proposed "a total reconstruction of sciences, arts, and all human knowledge" so as to master the world's resources. But first, addressing himself to the mood of his time, Bacon grapples with the spirit of Dürer's *Melencolia.* He considers at some length "why men despair," as he says, "and think things impossible." But then, urging us to "take state-prudence into our counsels" — to be good citizens, in other words — he turns from despair, "to speak touching hope." All our sorrows, he says in effect, must be turned to labor, to hard experimental study — of the kind recommended by Machiavelli, which turns knowledge into power.

From Machiavelli and Bacon, through Hobbes and Locke and Jean Jacques Rousseau, the talk of hope mounts in intensity. The method of experimental science, applied to politics and its material base by means of mental as well as physical models, raises man's confidence in his own rationality till he undertakes, as we saw, to wipe the slate of the past clean and make a new political beginning — first of all in France. Like experimenters in a chemist's or physicist's laboratory, the state-crafters of the French Revolution

"MELENCOLIA"
(Albrecht Dürer)

SIR FRANCIS BACON
(1561-1626)

NAGASAKI, 1945

went about their work methodically, counting the heads they meant to lop off and the institutions they meant to uproot before laying the experimental foundations for their new society.

We mentioned how history responded to such presumption. And we named the two great figures of the next age, one a systematic philosopher, the other a tireless revolutionary, who accorded history her due, as no one else before them had ever done.

Europe's New Aristotle

G. W. F. Hegel was not a Prussian. Stuttgart, where he was born in 1770 and educated till he was 18, was then the capital of the Duchy of Würtenburg, which didn't become a part of the German Empire until 1871. Hegel completed his university studies at Tübingen and then taught at the universities of Jena, Heidelburg, and Berlin, where he died in 1831. His major writings include the famous *Phenomenology of Mind* — his so-called journey of despair — published in 1807: a work that powerfully influenced Karl Marx a generation later, especially the chapter on "Lordship and Bondage," which gave Marx his profoundest revolutionary insights. This was followed by a massive two-volume *Science of Logic,* published in 1816, in which the notorious method of the Hegelian dialectic is pursued analytically through every conceivable idea, from that of mere *being,* undistinguishable (as the ancient Hindus knew) from *nothing,* to the highest idea of *God,* whom the Greeks, and especially Aristotle, identified as *thought thinking thought,* in its absolute fullness.

What his intention was in philosophy, Hegel finally revealed in 1817, with the publication, in three volumes, of his *Encyclopedia of the Philosophical Sciences.* It was to provide the basis, as Hegel explains, for a complete synthesis of all knowledge such as Aristotle himself might have attempted had he lived to complete the systematic exposition of his thought on the design broadly sketched in several notable passages of the *Ethics, Politics,* and *Metaphysics.* The first volume of Hegel's *Encyclopedia* was a short version of his *Logic;* the second, a *Philosophy of Nature,* divided into the mechanical, empirical-physical, and biological sciences; and the third, a *Philosophy of Mind,* integrating the one-sided "truths" of abstract logic and phenomenal nature in the higher developmental rationality of what Hegel calls the *subjective, objective,* and *absolute* (divine) phases of the growth of human spirit. The subjective sciences of mind are anthropology, phenomenology, and psychology; under objective mind are included the sciences of abstract right, or law, subjective right, or morality, economics (in the Greek sense of the term, which means the science of household management), political-economy, sociology, politics, and history; and under absolute mind are included the study of fine art, of religion in the most inclusive sense, and, finally, an ultimate synthesis in the highest reaches of philosophy.

Many of these human, social, and cultural sciences of the third part of the *Encyclopedia* Hegel elaborated at great length in later writings and lectures. In 1821, three years after Karl Marx was born, he published his major book on ethics, political economy, and politics, titled the *Philosophy of Right.* Marx later devoured every paragraph of this book, writing endless commentaries and criticisms. And so did Lenin, much later. The large section on political economy contains all the basic ideas about the internal development of capitalism that we usually associate with Marx, as well as the ideas about capitalist imperialism that we usually associate with Lenin. But it also contains notions of a corporate state such as we find in the anticommunist, co-organic political philosophies of Benedetto Croce, Bernard Bosanquet, and William Yandell Elliott, as well as in the liberal welfare-state philosophies of Herbert Croly and John Dewey.

The *Philosophy of Right,* it has been said, is a vast ocean in which all kinds of political thinkers, left, right, and

HEGEL MEDALLION

KARL MARX (1818-1883)
(Highgate Cemetery, London)

center, have very profitably dipped their buckets. Through Marx and Lenin, but directly too, it is proving itself to be the most influential book on politics ever written. After he published it, Hegel devoted his chief intellectual labors to his year-long series of lectures on the philosophies of history, fine art, and religion, and on the history of philosophy, transcriptions of which now fill twelve volumes of his collected works.

On Hegel's 60th birthday — in 1830, the year before he died — some of his students, who were already teachers themselves and even statesmen of some reputation, presented him with a medallion. On one side is the philosopher's head in profile, with his name and "From His Students" inscribed around it. The other side sums up his students' impression of what Hegel had sought to achieve as a modern Aristotle. The male figure in a flowing classical robe, seated on the left, with a large open book on his lap, has above him the wide-eyed owl of Minerva, symbol of the classical Greek spirit which seeks after wisdom. The female figure, similarly draped, confronts the wise man with a large cross, sign of the preachers of Christianity, of the Messiah crucified, which was — as St. Paul said — unto the Jews a stumbling block, and unto the Greeks foolishness.

Between these two representations of the chief ancient legacies of Western civilization (which Matthew Arnold will distinguish as Hellenism and Hebraism) stands a youthful winged figure, with arms extended to link the two. When he saw the medallion, Germany's chief poet, Goethe, was shocked and displeased. But there is no doubt that Hegel warmly appreciated this attempt to express his absorption of the stumbling-block of the Cross — of the total self-alienation of God — in his profoundest historical and philosophical teachings.

Marx and Minerva's Owl

The significance of Minerva's owl is, of course, familiar to all who have read more than a page of Marx's passionate rejection of the traditional ideal of the dispassionate pursuit of truth. In its briefest form that rejection now serves as Marx's epitaph, his final word to all who come to look upon his grave in London's Highgate Cemetery. There, beneath his monumental bust, are inscribed the words: "Philosophers have only *interpreted* the world in various ways; the point, however, is to *change* it."

The French revolutionary thinkers of the 18th century had tried to change man's world from top to bottom, without studying its history. Marx didn't make their mistake. Under Hegel's influence, he learned to appreciate that history has an inner reason of its own, and that, even if one hates it all and wishes to destroy it, he had better study it, to learn its inner laws. Yet if one's heart is filled with hatred, if one approaches history to discover its laws the way a thief might try to discover the combination of someone else's safe, in order to make off with the contents, the result is not apt to be anything resembling that pure love of wisdom which the Greeks called *philosophia*. Marx's purpose in studying history was, as he said, to turn his knowledge into power, and to use that power experimentally to destroy it all and build something totally different. Different in what way? It didn't really matter. What mattered was to destroy what *is*. Early in his revolutionary career, when he was mapping out his life's program, Marx wrote about himself and his revolutionary friends:

> We do not attempt dogmatically to prefigure the future, but want to find the new world only through criticism of the old . . . . What we have to accomplish in the present is a ruthless criticism of everything existing, ruthless in two senses: the criticism must not be afraid of its own conclusions, nor of conflict with the powers that be.

Although Marx quite parasitically adopted Hegel's method of criticism, the method of the dialectic, his application of it was the very opposite of Hegel's. Hegel, Marx would soon be saying, has to be turned upside down, like the world of national cultures he defended. All that Hegel represents as true in politics must be declared false, and all that Hegel exalts — like art, religion, and philosophy — must be brought crashing down, to be buried under the ruins of the political systems that have made art, religion, and philosophy historically possible.

In saying that the important thing is not to interpret the world but to *change* it, Marx had in mind this often-quoted passage at the beginning of Hegel's *Philosophy of Right,* where Hegel says; "As for teaching what *ought to be* in this world, philosophy, in any event, always comes on the scene too late for that." Not philosophy, not scholarly study, but "passions, private aims, and the satisfaction of selfish desires," Hegel explains, "are the most effective springs of action in human history." Why? "Because passions and selfish aims exert a more direct influence over men," says Hegel, "than the discipline that tends toward order and self-restraint, law and morality."

It is exciting to engage in a ruthless criticism of everything existing; and it is even more exciting to hack one's way up to the top of a revolutionary dictatorship with a monopoly of power to crush all one has criticized and hated. Yet, when we read the historical record of what such passions and ambitions have wrought, when we contemplate the "miseries that have overwhelmed the noblest nations and polities, and the finest examples of private virtue," we experience, Hegel writes, "mental torture allowing no defense or escape but the consideration that what has happened could not be otherwise." It is out of a history that "excites emotions of the profoundest and most hopeless sadness," says Hegel, in the spirit of the *Melencolia,* that we pass beyond economics and politics, and even beyond history, into the sphere of true wisdom in the Greek and Christian sense.

"True wisdom, as the thought of the world," Hegel continues, "does not appear until reality has already shaped itself completely and is hardening in its mold." The transition to wisdom, then, is the flight of Minerva's owl, which is possible only when the long day's task is done. True philosophy's backward glance on the wreckage of political history is not a ruthless new contribution to further wreckage. On the contrary, when we study history for the sake of truth, what we gain is a tragic insight into its necessity — an insight that purges the soul of its fear and pity and other passions, so that it can at last begin to be free, like God, in absolute self-knowledge.

The Global Legacy of the Nations

The highest activity of free mind is self-critical, not self-righteous or self-complacent. Excited by doubt, free mind, purged by historical study, brings its critical quest for truth to focus first of all, says Hegel,

> on its own social environment: which is to say, on the institutions and forms of government of the people among whom subjective mind has emancipated itself through self-knowledge and makes its appearance as free. It focuses its critical powers on their morality, their social life and capabilities, customs and enjoyments; their attempts and achievements in art and science; their religious experience; their foreign relations and wars; and, lastly, the origins and progress of the states arising to displace them.

That is Hegel's own summary of what he attempted to do in all his published books and lectures, but especially in his writings and lectures on phenomenology, politics, history, art, religion, and philosophy. Always his basic approach is developmental. Against the *philosophes* who imagined they could think themselves free of history by ignoring it, he demonstrates quite unanswerably that the attitude of rationalistic enlightenment is itself manifestly a child of history, apart from which it could never have come to be. Yet in every field that Hegel approached historically, his influence, it needs to be stressed, has been not that of a backward-looking antiquarian but of a trailblazer. "We may be critically inclined toward this Hegelian heritage,"

Professor Carl Friedrich of Harvard has written, "but we cannot gainsay its influence." Hegel's "insistence on the unity of culture is now so widely accepted that it is difficult to believe that it was once a revolutionary principle." Its impact on social activists and artists, as well as philosophers, has been "so all-engulfing," Friedrich concludes, that to survey it "would fall little short of an intellectual history of the century [and a half] since his death."

Hegel, we need to recall, not only reminded his anti-historical contemporaries of the importance of their own national histories, he did more than anyone else to open up the cultures of the Near and Far East to them also. How fresh this aspect of Hegel's influence remains is attested to, for instance, by the most eminent cultural archeologist of our time, W. F. Albright. In his classic volume, *From the Stone Age to Christianity: Monotheism and the Historical Process,* Albright reminds his readers that it was Hegel who, for the first time, "brought together the data of history in a rational synthesis, exhibiting the progress of humanity from its Asiatic cradle to modern Western Europe and clearly recognizing the fact of cultural evolution"; and then he explicitly acknowledges that his own approach to the artistic-religious legacies of the peoples of the ancient Near East is Hegelian, including his interpretations of the verses of the Old and New Testaments.

Kurt F. Leidecker, a contemporary specialist in the art and philosophy of India, makes a similar point, stressing especially the importance of Hegel's method in his field. Modern research has of course brought to light much factual material about the Far East that Hegel could not have known; yet there was in Hegel's method, says Leidecker, an element "so oriental in itself," that its value to scholars increases as their particularized knowledge increases. "The dialectic," he concludes, "is the greatest and permanent achievement of Hegel and it was the trailblazer for the synthesis between Orient and Occident."

Summing up this aspect of Hegel's influence,

Edmund Scherer, the French critic so highly praised by
Irving Babbitt in his *Masters of Modern French Criticism,* does
not hesitate to say:

> Hegel has taught us the respect and intelligence of the facts.
> Through him we know that what was and is must have its
> reason, its justification in itself . . . . That is the strength of
> Hegel's study and criticism. And what a marvelous under-
> standing of the past we have in consequence. How it lives
> again before our eyes! The affiliations of peoples, the
> advance of civilizations, the character of different times,
> the genius of languages, the sense of mythologies, the
> inspiration of national poetries, the essence of religions . .
> . . It is of the very essence of things that a truth is complete
> only insofar as its contrary is introduced into it, to rise
> afterwards to a higher conciliation.

Aristotle, as we noted, had said that the peoples of
Asia were too easily organizable on a massive scale, too
ready to submit to absolutist rule for the sake of peace,
whereas the peoples of the West and North were, on the
contrary, perhaps too free, too ungovernable for civilized
life. The Greeks, in between, were a mixture of the two,
part free, like the Westerners, part servile, like the peoples
of the East. In his lectures on the history of philosophy as
on the philosophy of history, art, and religion, Hegel
develops a similar view. After a long study of classical
culture, Eastern culture, and his own Western culture, he
comes to the conclusion that the history of mankind, from
the establishment of the earliest civilizations, has been the
history of the progress of political and individual freedom.
In the ancient East, the only form of freedom ever attained
was the political kind that a people enjoys *as a whole* when
it has been forcibly united by a benign despot. In Greece
and Rome, a large measure of *individual* freedom was
added to the freedom of political unity, especially when
there were literally thousands of small but free city-states.
The late Roman Empire appeared to have collapsed back
into oriental despotism for the sake of peace. But, as Hegel
stresses, under that despotic imperial rule something new

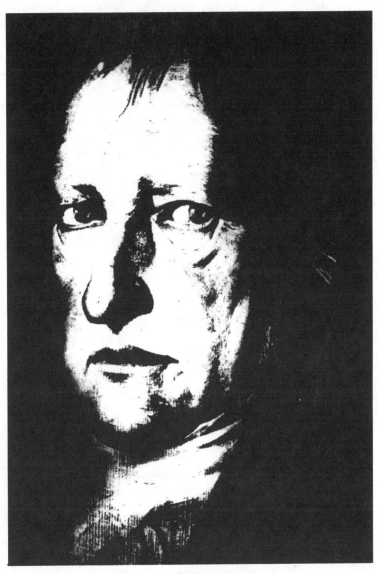

GEORG W. F. HEGEL
(1770-1831)

ABRAHAM LINCOLN (1809-1865)
(Lincoln Memorial, Washington, D.C.)

was added: a sense of spiritual identity that tended to separate the individual conscience from the bonds of merely temporal community.

That new sense of individuality had come into the Greco-Roman world from the Jews, in the form of Christianity, and it was destined to survive the collapse of that world. In fact, when Aristotle's ungovernable Northwest Europeans conquered Rome, they found the new spiritual individuality of the Christian conscience extraordinarily compatible with their native sense of independence; and the fusion of the two made them capable, in time, of governing themselves politically with an unprecedented high measure of individual freedom for all.

The result in the West has been a world not of vast despotic states including many nations, and not of single nations divided into many little states. Those two opposed principles of antiquity, both based on slavery, are reconciled in the modern world's ideal of the nation-state, each single member of which, as an individual, is actually or potentially free, according to the measure of perfection of the national union. Our own country is typical. As all the world knows, it was originally not only a slave society but also a very *imperfect* national union, divided politically into many states. The man who as President emancipated its slaves also made it a more perfect national union. The words above the somber portrayal of him, in a mood the antithesis of that of Marx, read:

> In this temple as in the hearts of the people for whom he saved the Union the memory of Abraham Lincoln is enshrined forever.

For the safety of his people, this new Abraham, like the old one, had been prepared to make an awful sacrifice — and, tragically, his hand could not be stayed.

Marx or Hegel?

Our Civil War was a forge of nationhood. Although Hegel died a generation before its start, his writings and lectures on the progress of freedom cast a powerful light upon it. Marx, on the contrary, lived through both the war and the period of reconstruction (he died in 1883); but for him it had no intrinsic meaning, since, while he despised the South, he also envisioned no future for unions of the kind that Lincoln had saved for the American people. After Lincoln's death, the Northern capitalist leaders had broken with his plan to heal the nation's wounds as quickly as possible; and this they had done by subjecting the conquered South to the worst kind of economic exploitation imaginable. Yet Marx had only praise for that sort of capitalist greed, which served admirably, in his view, to destroy national differences and national attachments, thereby preparing the way, without knowing it, for the "inevitable" triumph of communism.

Thus, by harnessing the force of the class-struggle under capitalism, the communist revolutionaries would in effect be merely completing the job of de-nationalizing mankind started by capitalism. When it is in full gear, the revolution will bring the Western governments down one after another, till the moment is ripe historically for the imposition of an absolutely "final" solution to all the world's ills. The one indispensable thing in the end, according to Marx, will be a monopoly of coercive power concentrated for a relatively short time in the right hands — the hands of alien-minded revolutionaries like himself. The government they imposed would not be a government in the traditional sense. It would not prepare the ruled to rule in turn. On the contrary, it would discipline and train them till they ceased to desire to rule in turn, at which time the very need to rule would wither away. Only the Marxist revolutionary leaders who organized the class-struggle — a select few — would ever have to bear the burden of ruling others. The depoliticized masses living under the last political regime before the communist millenium would never have to bear the awful responsibility of ruling anybody, least of all themselves.

Marx's scheme here is really nothing more nor less than a *hateful* parody of what he found in the pages of Hegel's *Philosophy of Right* devoted to what Hegel calls the "dialectic of civil society" — the dialectic of capitalist expansion. According to Hegel, the class struggle at the heart of that economic dialectic is a politically educative struggle. When capitalism learns that it cannot prevent poverty in the midst of plenty at home, it carries its private enterprise *overseas*. And this overseas expansion, in so far as it is protected by national power, is already a step beyond the purely economic sphere into politics. Overseas, without intending it, capitalist enterprise has the effect of transforming the ways of living of great masses of people. Colonial conquests, wars of economic rivalry, are an inevitable result. But in the process, entire populations that had been socially static are suddenly overtaken by the discontents of rising expectations. And that has tremendous political consequences both at home and abroad. The day inevitably comes when economic frontiers close, and even the most rugged of economic individualists is forced to recognize the need for statecraft. Colonies then declare their political independence, if they can; and even where they cannot, the level of political consciousness is steadily raised in land after land.

Only in the modern world, Hegel stresses, have the economic tensions of civil society become global in extent, thereby raising all classes in all lands, finally, to political consciousness. The spirit of those virtually ungovernable Northwest Europeans that Aristotle had spoken of has made this global transformation possible. Thus the progress of freedom passes into its final world-historic phase. Throughout the world, political government now becomes, gradually but inexorably, a matter not merely for despots, as in the East, where traditionally only *one* has ever been really free; and not merely for certain classes of privileged birth and education, as in Greece and Rome and the formative centuries of Western Europe, where *some* have been free. All that is past. As a consequence of the dialectic of civil society, political government has now become, at least potentially, a matter for the participation of all, without exception — once all, as citizens, have been raised to equality in freedom in the "more perfect union" of a modern nation-state. As the system of nation-states extends itself around the globe, each people in its separate and equal station as a member of that system will get its chance for a self-governed advance in science, art, religion, and philosophy, as well as economics. That is Hegel's vision of the world's future; and it is, of course, the opposite of what Marx projected.

The "Positive Humanism" of Karl Marx

But what exactly did Marx project? His chief apologists in the West now insist that he was not a mere economic revolutionary, that his real concern was rather to *overcome* economics, and thereby inaugurate an age of what he called "Positive Humanism." Communism, we are told, is only one side of positive humanism — its economic, utilitarian side. Atheism makes up its anti-religious, ethical side, while cosmopolitanism makes up its anti-national cultural side.

Working in tandem, revolutionary communism, atheism, and cosmopolitanism will transform this dull old world into an aesthetic utopia. When capitalism's age-old division of labor is finally abolished by the communist dictatorship, says Marx in a famous passage of his *German Ideology*, it will be possible for me, for instance,

> to do one thing today and another tomorrow, to hunt in the morning, fish in the afternoon, rear cattle in the evening, and criticize after dinner, just as I have a mind, without ever becoming hunter, fisherman, shepherd, or critic.

There will be an end to the "concentration of artistic talent in particular individuals and its suppression in the broad mass." The traditional "subordination of the artist to local and national narrowness" will cease, as will also his "subordination to some definite art, thanks to which he is exclusively a painter, sculptor, etc., the very name of his activity adequately expressing the narrowness of his professional development and his dependence on division of labor. In a communist society there are no painters but at most people who, among other activities, also engage in painting, etc."

The people Marx speaks of as populating his aesthetic utopia of positive humanism will of course be people without nationalities, without religions, without traditionally-shaped artistic or political identities: "Sans teeth" — one is tempted to say with Shakespeare's Jacques — "sans eyes, sans taste, sans anything."

Alexander Solzhenitsyn's anguished cry against such cultural nihilism has been heard around the world. But in Marx's own time it was the Zionist Jews who first directly felt its destructive impact. We all know something of Marx's pathetically hateful attitude toward what he called the twin opiates of Jewish nationalism and religious fervor. But we need perhaps to be reminded that, in saying *no* to Marx, the leading Zionists of the day often turned to Hegel for an effective antidote. In an article titled "Hegel and Judaism," the eminent Jewish scholar Emil Fackenheim has touched on this matter of early Zionist attitudes toward Hegel. Asking whether any modern philosophy can do justice to the Jewish cultural perspective, so sharply criticized by Marx, he does not hesitate to say that Hegel's system "is perhaps, of all philosophies, the *only one* capable of doing so." Fackenheim then discusses the elements in Hegel's thought that clearly define "a future for the Jewish people in the modern world, the dialectical [Marxist] dissipation of their religious past notwithstanding," and he concludes that those elements lend "more than poetic truth to the fact that the first Western Zionist philosophy — that of Moses Hess — was largely Hegelian."

Largely Hegelian, too, because it comes straight

out of Moses Hess, is what the distinguished Israeli statesman Abba Eban has said in protesting the anti-Israeli
attitudes of supra-nationalist critics, whether in Moscow,
London, or New York. In his *Voice of Israel,* for instance, he
reminds such critics that "the original revelations of human culture have come not out of vast continental empires, but out of small, coherent, and well-articulated small
states." And as for the claims that history has now passed
the sovereign nation-states by, Eban replies in this thoroughly Hegelian vein:

> The eclipse of nationalism by some supra-national feder-
> alism has been predicted so often that it is one of the
> platitudes of twentieth century writing. But, in fact, this
> century is the triumphant epoch of the nation-state, and
> the burial ground of broader associations and groupings
> . . . . The idea of a system of sovereign states confronting
> each other within the framework of equal obligations is
> the most progressive that the human mind can conceive.
> Just as it would be reactionary to abolish those distinc-
> tions of language, literature, and art, which give to the
> human mind its infinite variety, so it would be retro-
> grade to abolish the political sovereignties of peoples.

Those words echo closely what Hegel wrote over a
hundred and fifty years ago about the "individuality" of
nations once they have attained a "more perfect union" of
their citizens so that they might more effectively assume a
"separate and equal station" among the powers of the
earth. "Individuality," said Hegel,

> is awareness of one's existence as a unit in sharp distinc-
> tion from others. It manifests itself on the level of the
> state as a relation to other states, each of which is
> autonomous *vis-a-vis* the others. This autonomy embod-
> ies mind's actual awareness of itself as a unit and hence
> it is the most fundamental freedom which a people
> possesses as well as its highest dignity . . . . Those who talk
> of the "wishes" of a "collection" of people to renounce its
> own political center and autonomy in order to unite with
> others to form a new whole, have very little knowledge of

what a "collection" is or of the feeling of selfhood which a nation possesses in its independence.

Unlike Solzhenitsyn, Abba Eban, or Hegel, Marx looked with absolute hatred upon all that gave peoples their national identities, freedom, and dignity. The best thing for the Jews, he declared, was to disappear historically. In any event, the Communist Revolution would certainly "put an end to anti-Semitism," he insisted, by smashing the bourgeois classes in which it festers, and "the Jews would then disappear into the proletariat." As for the gentile "nations," Marx was even more confident that their working classes would welcome the destruction of all national ties and allegiances. In this expectation, with respect to both Jews and Gentiles, Marx was, as we shall see, grossly mistaken.

III. TOMORROW'S WORLD OF
FREE NATIONS

The period of a century and a half that preceded the French Revolution in Europe is often called the Age of Enlightenment. But that is a misnomer. For what happened during that period was not an awakening of cultural self-consciousness, but rather the very opposite. Just as, in the Renaissance, the peoples of Western Europe tried to forget who they actually were by imitating the Romans and Greeks, so in the 18th century they again tried to forget who they were by living according to precepts of abstract reasoning, as if they had never had a real history.

Only when abstract reasoning had obviously failed did a genuinely enlightened awakening of the historic sense occur. The commandment of enlightenment is as we said: Know thyself. And to really know themselves, the modern European peoples had finally to study seriously the history of their national formation in the Christian Middle Ages — during the centuries of the Germanic tribal conquests of ancient Rome, of the empire of Charlemagne, of feudalism, of the Crusades, of commercial communes, of Gothic cathedrals, of Giotto's paintings and Dante's poetry, and of the great monarchic feudal "houses" that gradually transformed themselves into monarchic states.

Before the dawn of the Romantic Era, we really know the Western European peoples historically only from the outside, from the standpoint of foreigners. We have several times cited Aristotle's appraisal of them, which is the earliest objective appraisal we have. He said, you will recall, that they were excessively spirited and therefore

"THE CONSPIRACY OF CLAUDIUS CIVILIS"
(Rembrandt)

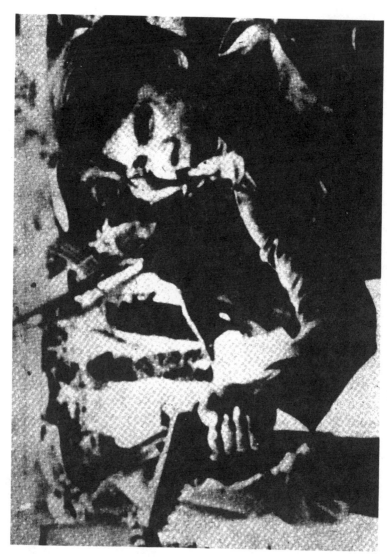

SOUTHEAST ASIA (April 17, 1945)

virtually ungovernable. Julius Caesar, who sought to pacify
them on the northern borders of the Roman Empire,
agreed. Then it is the Roman historian Tacitus, writing in
the first century B.C., who gives us a somewhat clearer
picture of them in his little book titled *Germania*. This is
followed by Roman Christian representations and later by
medieval Roman Catholic representations — always viewing them from the outside, from a foreign, not a native
perspective. Not until after the Reformation, when many
of them have abruptly turned their backs on the maternal
care of the Church, do we get the beginnings of anything
resembling self-portraiture in the literature and art of the
Northwest Europeans. And even then, as we said, abstract
reasoning is invoked to gloss over the most striking pecu-
liarities.

"Freedom-Fighters" Against Rome

At one point in his *Germania* Tacitus had told the story of
the first freedom-fighter of the old Germanic Batavians,
whose modern descendants are the Dutch. Because of
mismanagement by local bureaucrats, a tribe of Batavians
hired by the Romans to patrol their northern borders had
risen in revolt. Events moved quickly. The Roman bureaucrats on the scene had been slain. But when Roman back-
up forces arrived, the uprising was quelled and its leader
driven off into an obscurity from which he never emerged.
Tacitus's attitude in narrating the events is very like what
will be the attitude of many Europeans toward American
Indians in the 18th century: free of civilized vices, the
Batavians he portrays have a touch of noble savagery to
redeem them, even in revolt.

Well, sixteen hundred years after Tacitus, the modern Batavians, running a vast empire of their own, and
maintaining great universities that received the most learned
scholars of the world, decided it was time to honor the first
Dutchman who had ever raised a sword of protest against
tyranny emanating from Rome. In the 17th century, the

Calvinist Dutch had just come out of an eighty-year success-
ful revolt against the Catholic Kings of Spain. So they
called on the greatest painter. of the time, Rembrandt, to
paint a grand historical canvas for them, to be called "The
Conspiracy of Claudius Civilis" — of Claudius the "true
citizen" — for that was the Latin name the Batavian chief
had assumed in the Roman service. Those who commissioned the painting had apparently expected Rembrandt
to give them a hero in their own likeness: neat and orderly
and business-like, raising a civilized sword against oppressive Roman government.

But Rembrandt, gave them instead a portrait of
conspirators anything but neat and orderly. When it was
unveiled, the burgomasters of Amsterdam who commissioned it were shocked; and Pieter Geyl, one of the leading
Dutch cultural historians of our time, explains why.
"Rembrandt knew how to render the primitive and the
savage," he writes.

> The barbaric, the vigorous, the passionate — in the
> countenances and in the attitudes of the plotters who
> crowd about the table lighted up by torches in the vast
> dark room — it has all been grippingly evoked, and the
> effect is embodied in the mighty one-eyed figure, who,
> sturdily and fatefully seated, holds his sword aloft, while
> the others touch it with theirs. That blunt presentation
> of the first Dutch warrior for freedom apparently of-
> fended the chastened convention of the burgomasters of
> Amsterdam.

Though it had been commissioned, the painting was rejected. And so the large central fragment which alone
survives now hangs not anywhere in Holland but in the
museum at Stockholm! Professor Geyl continues:

> Modern historic, no less than artistic awareness, will
> unhesitatingly recognize the veracity of Rembrandt's
> fantasy. Everyone can see at once that his are the authen-
> tically desperate conspirators and that they are moved by
> very different passions from those the painter might

have observed around him in the erudite and decent burghers of Amsterdam, familiar with the pen and the account book and the law court.

To give us a more vivid literary sense of what Rembrandt achieved, Geyl concludes:

Macbeth's banquet, at which Banquo's ghost horrifies Macbeth and Macbeth's terror disconcerts his guests, might have been painted by the same hand.

The burgomasters of Amsterdam in Rembrandt's time had simply not been prepared to look at their distant past realistically. And two centuries had to pass before the historic insight of a Rembrandt could be fully appreciated. Think how different our attitudes are today. All around the world, but especially in ex-colonial areas, we now see swords, or other more fashionable weapons, being raised by freedom-fighters quite in the style of Rembrandt's representation. The news reports in our time remind us, in other words, that we must not expect a uniform march of civilization into the future. Each people has its specific identity and its specific time. What suits the Dutch or English today can hardly suit the Mallacans or Mallayans, any more than what suited the Romans in Tacitus's time could have suited the Batavians of Rembrandt's Claudius Civilis.

Stages of Political Growth

We speak today of old, new, and emergent nation-states. But it would be a mistake, of course, to assume that the old are all equally old, the new all equally new, or the emergent all emerging simultaneously at an equal pace. In their *Communist Manifesto* of 1848, Marx and Engels stressed the fact that different societies are in different stages of economic growth; that some are still in a feudal stage of a subsistence-economy or just entering the capitalist stage, while others are so far advanced in the capitalist stage that they seem ripe for revolution and the ushering in of a communist party dictatorship. Still, it was Marx's view, as we saw, that capitalism was fast homogenizing the world, that its rapid expansion would soon destroy what made Frenchmen French, Englishmen English, etc., as surely as it would provoke proletarian uprisings to destroy private ownership of the means of production and the classes profiting by it.

But it is clear that, viewing things as an outsider in Germany, Belgium, France, and England, Marx misread the signs of the times on nationalism. Throughout his life he failed to recognize the obvious fact that, as a rule, the expression of national feeling is apparently weakest in old nations that can take their national unity for granted and that it is apt to be strongest where achievement of sovereign nationhood seems to have been forcibly prevented by others. At one extreme was England, with national unity so strongly inbred ("We few, we *happy* few"!) that there could be no question about it in anyone's mind who felt any love at all for the country. Though he spent forty years in England, Marx, who had no such love, failed to see this. He saw only that there was nothing in England of the sort of "agitation" for national unity that was then animating the supporters of Cavour and Mazzini in divided Italy, or of Bismarck in Germany, or of Lincoln in America, where a few years later the national union would be put on trial by an all-out war between the states. One doesn't agitate for what one has.

Not that Germany, Italy, or America approaching the Civil War were extreme cases. In Eastern Europe, for instance, there were nations wholly absorbed in vast empires like those of the Russian Czars, Austria-Hungary, and the Ottoman Turks. Still other national groups, like the Poles, were divided politically so as to be shared by two or three neighboring multinational states. And finally there was the enduring national plight of the Jews, for whom the task of shaping or recovering a united nationhood was plainly the most difficult of all and therefore the most compellingly-felt of all.

Marx's notion that capitalist expansion would ho-
mogenize all these peoples was of course as historically
baseless as the 18th century notion that national, political,
religious, and cultural particularities could simply be rea-
soned away. In fact, after 1848, England was perhaps the
only country in the world where it could sound at all
reasonable to suggest that there might one day actually be
a nationless, stateless, classless world-community of the
kind envisioned by the 18th century rationalists, with their
abstract social-contract theory, and by Marx, with his anti-
nationalist historical materialism. Precisely because England could take its national unity for granted, it could be
tolerant on this score. What kept England strong in the
world was not much theorized about till the end of the
century. The men who pursued the nation's abiding interests at home and abroad did so quietly, for the most part.
In contrast, what was heard loudly, what attracted the
interest of radical and "progressive" thinkers abroad, was
usually the exceptional talk of a few notable mavericks,
who liked to speak of human liberty as if they had in mind
each and every human being on the face of the earth, when
in fact what they said actually applied almost exclusively to
the particular status of Englishmen in England at that time.

Generalizing on the characteristically English political insights of Hobbes and Locke, these internationally
famous but exceptional English thinkers of the 19th century pressed the old argument that government was necessary, basically, only to get an excessively free and spirited
people to cooperate initially. For that purpose, conquest
made a good start. It could be conquest from abroad, as in
England in 1066; or it could be conquest from within, with
one domestic group or class imposing its will on others, as
in the English-American colonies after 1776, or in
Bismarck's Germany. But once unity has been forcibly
established, and the people have begun to appreciate and
enjoy its benefits, then the unifying government should, it
was argued, gradually relax and diminish its application of

force.

England's Spare Chancellor: Walter Bagehot

But how far should the relaxation of the use of governmental force be allowed to go in a well-ordered modern community? The history of 19th century English political thought is in large measure a history of the answers given to that question first of all by the old utilitarians, then by liberal reformers and libertarian individualists, and finally by the so-called Fabian or evolutionary socialists. Yet, before speaking of any of these, we want to dwell for a moment on an exceptionally able man who falls under none of these designations, though he gives each of them its due in his writings, while according similar treatment to the altogether different aspirations of Bismarckian and Mazzinian nationalists, American Unionists, Zionists, and even neo-Marxists of the caliber of Lenin, who will later "invert" Marx, as Marx had earlier proposed to invert Hegel.

The man I speak of is Walter Bagehot [pronounced BADGE-ut] — an economist, merchant-fleet owner, banker, journalist, expert on the constitutional systems of the United States and England, and literary critic of the first rank. He is the man who first made the London *Economist* the great financial magazine it has since remained. Everyone in England who writes about the English Parliamentary system of government and everyone in America who writes on the American Presidential system of government is greatly in his debt. He lived at the time of our Civil War, which was also the time of the unification of Italy and Germany and of the political transformation of England by a series of virtually revolutionary reform bills.

What Bagehot did was to trace a pattern of historical development that assigned a suitable place for every sort of economic, social, political, historic, aesthetic, religious, and philosophic aspiration known to contemporary man. With respect to alternative futures in politics he

WALTER BAGEHOT
(1826-1877)

BISMARCK
(1815-1898)

CAVOUR
(1810-1861)

observed that, for the foreseeable future, the chief forms of government available to mankind would remain basically *four*. They are the traditional or hereditary form, which is apt to be stable because succession is determined by birth, but also inefficient for the same reason, since birth cannot guarantee competence. Opposed to this at the opposite extreme, is the revolutionary form of government, either of charismatic dictators or dictatorial oligarchic elites. This is apt to be unstable but efficient, since dictators usually last only so long as they remain too efficiently clever to let themselves be overthrown.

In between these essentially involuntary traditional and dictatorial forms of government lies a whole range of more or less voluntary forms, of which, in the contemporary world — so says Bagehot — those of the United States and England are most representative. In the Introduction to his classic study of the English and American Constitutions, Bagehot writes:

> I do not apologize for dwelling at length upon these points, for the subject is one of transcendent importance. The practical choice of first-rate nations is between the presidential government and the parliamentary; no state can be first-rate which has not a government by discussion, and those are the only two existing species of that government. It is between them that a nation which has to choose in government must choose.

Yet no people, not the English, not the Americans, can *begin* with such a government. Bagehot proceeds to explain what the beginning must be like. And here he contrasts himself sharply with Marx. For while he observes the same hard facts about class struggle and coercive government, he brings to his study of those facts a mind filled not with hatred and revolutionary schemes but with the most comprehensive political ideas that have been available to Western thinkers from the time of Plato and Aristotle and Polybius, through that of St. Augustine, St. Thomas, and Machiavelli, and beyond, to Hobbes, Locke,

Rousseau, the authors of the Federalist papers, and Tocqueville.

In the pattern of historical development of nations that Bagehot defines, the beginning is some kind of forced unity applying a bond of law, regardless of the content of that law. All that matters is that the law be obeyed collectively. Whatever its internal character, such unity gives a people a tremendous advantage over neighbors who are divided. Yet it can continue to be advantageous, says Bagehot, only if it gradually gains the consent of the governed, so that less and less force needs to be used to get citizens to obey the law. For most peoples, obedience then becomes customary or traditional, supported more by education than by force.

Consent earned for *forced* unity makes it *felt* unity. This kind of felt unity is not to be confused with tribal feeling, which is pre-political. Most modern states have not been formed by a single tribe or people, but rather by two or more peoples. Needless to say, the forced unity of two distinct peoples is anything but a tribal unity to begin with; therefore, when it becomes *felt*, like that of the Normans and Anglo-Saxons in England, it is something altogether new: a unity not tribal, but political and national in the purest sense, fusing at least two, and often many more, pre-national tribal feelings.

But here again, the advantages of felt unity can be enjoyed for long only if the feeling doesn't harden, doesn't become inflexible and exclusive. If felt unity develops too thick a crust of custom, the emerging national spirit suffocates. By preventing the formation of such a crust, or by breaking it quickly when it has formed, a people passes into a higher stage of civilized political life — that of *government by discussion*.

Governments by discussion are based on the prior stages of forced and felt unity — stages which cannot be skipped and the potentials of which must be preserved in the higher stage. For, as Bagehot warns:

History is strewn with the wrecks of nations which have gained a little progressiveness at the cost of a great deal of hard manliness, and have thus prepared themselves for destruction as soon as the movements of the world gave a chance for it.

From Spencer and Mill to Lenin and Wilson

When he wrote those words, Bagehot was fully aware of what utilitarians like James Mill, liberals like James' son John Stuart, and rugged-individualist libertarians like Herbert Spencer had in mind for English society. Long before Marx, liberal Englishmen had argued that, in the long run, the government that governs least governs best. The novelty of Herbert Spencer's thought, expressed as early as 1842 in *The Proper Sphere of Government* and as late as 1884 in *The Man Versus the State*, was the idea that, when and if people in England and elsewhere ever got really used to being absolutely free in a *lassaiz-faire* market place, the government that governs least would finally have nothing to do and would wither away.

John Stuart Mill had agreed generally with Spencer's view in this respect. But as the author of the famous essay *On Liberty*, concerned primarily with full freedom in the intellectual market place, he argued that the government, before withering away, ought to concentrate its remaining force on equalizing opportunities for intellectual cultivation. The dominant classes ought to do this eagerly, Mill believed, because it was ultimately in their own best interest. But, as he grew older, he also grew somewhat impatient. And he began to warn that if the dominant classes failed to act quickly, it might serve them right to be faced with a communist revolutionary uprising — a sort of thing which he otherwise wholly despised.

Out of Mill's position — despising communist revolutionary violence yet urging social reforms with something of a threat of violence to stimulate them — arose what has since come to be known as the Fabian movement of

English socialism, which corresponds to what is called evolutionary, or Bernsteinian socialism on the continent. Evolutionary socialists argued that socialists would have to gain control of the liberal state to get things done, but that such control should be gained by elective, not revolutionary means. The idea was to please Marx with socialist control of the government, Mill with the institution of reforms without recourse to violence, and eventually even Herbert Spencer, with a withering away of the state.

Needless to say, all of this liberal, libertarian, and evolutionary socialist convergence on the withering away of the state was a purely English phenomenon, having little relevance at all for peoples elsewhere who had yet to shape effective nation-state governments for themselves. Where the hard manliness of constructive statecraft — the statecraft of the stages of *forced* and *felt* political unity defined by Bagehot — is what is most urgently required for national well-being, talk of a state's eventual withering away, whether by Marxists or liberals, can count for little. Under the circumstances, Marxism might have faded off into oblivion, had it not occurred to some of the leading continental communists that Marx had got his basic priorities wrong.

Vladimir Ilyich Lenin, as we all know, did with Marx what Marx had purportedly done with Hegel. He turned him upside down. As the eminent Marxist scholar Y. S. Brenner explained it:

> Lenin accepted Marx's idea that "with the change in economic foundations, the entire immense superstructure [of culture, religion, philosophy, etc.] is more or less rapidly transformed," but he did to it what Marx had once done to Hegel's dialectic — he turned it upside down . . . . Marx had always looked upon the state as part of the social superstructure, as a dependent variable of [economic] growth. Lenin turned the state once again into an independent agent.

That is the most momentous thing that Lenin did. It transformed him from an alien-minded revolutionary

HERBERT SPENCER
(1820-1903)

JOHN STUART MILL
(1806-1873)

WOODROW WILSON
(1856-1924)

LENIN
(1870-1924)

ROOSEVELT (1882-1945) and
CHURCHILL (1874-1965)

MUSSOLINI (1883-1945) and
HITLER (1889-1945)

STALIN (1879-1953) and the
young KHRUSHCHEV (1894-1971)

CHIANG KAI-SHEK (1887-1975) and the
young MAO TSE-TUNG (1893-1976)

into the founding father, or builder, of a powerful nation-state with forced unity. Russia was not ripe for the Marxist-type communist takeover. Its society was not a rapidly expanding bourgeois capitalist society. But Lenin had learned the rule of statecraft which is as old as Aristotle. If you want to do anything on a large scale in this world, the necessary means — and therefore the first thing required — is not a theory of economics but a powerfully united state. Bismark, Cavour, Lincoln knew this. Lenin learned it, though he didn't get much of a chance to use it till the start of World War I, the first of the global wars fought by people determined to put an end to wars forever.

America went into World War I headed by a President who, as a professor of political science, had been Walter Bagehot's chief disciple in America. Woodrow Wilson had been an excellent student of American government, till he became President and eventually a global war leader. Then he forgot all he had learned from Bagehot. His one concern after 1914 was to introduce a "final solution" to all the world's ills at the end of the war. But the war that swept Wilson up to world leadership also swept up Lenin. And it is easy to see why such a man as Lenin was destined to exert a far more lasting influence on the world, for good or ill, than Wilson.

The Democratization of War

In the 1920s and 1930s, the big political news was made on the one hand by charismatic leader-types, either stabilizing their revolutionary governments, like Stalin, or creating them anew, like Hitler and Mussolini, or, on the other hand, by reformers and defenders of the world's chief governments by discussion. Two very eloquent men were charged to defend the Presidential and Cabinet forms of government against fascism in World War II. The first of them, Winston Churchill was something salvaged out of England's remoter past of forced and deeply-felt national unity. Franklin Roosevelt, on the other hand, had assembled around him at least as many innovative, future-oriented political theorists as surrounded Stalin, Mussolini, and Hitler.

Yet the ultimate significance of World War II is apt to be measured less in terms of men than of bombs. What if Germany had developed the atomic bomb before the United States? What if the Soviet Union had enjoyed a monopoly of control over atomic weapons for four years, after World War II?

It is enough to have to reckon with what in fact *is* in this sphere. What has political science to say about such weapons as the Soviet leaders, unlike our own, so proudly display in their principal squares? Our fallen President Nixon went to Red China to talk to Mao Tse Tung about those bombs. But he also journeyed to the Kremlin to toast the future with Brezhnev. Yet, what about the weapons themselves?

Surely there is only one adjective that can properly characterize weapons of such size and power. They are not monarchic weapons, fit only for kings — like that mighty sword that only King Arthur could pull out of a stone, by which feat he won acknowledgement as king of Britain. Neither are they aristocratic weapons, fit only for use by skilled and chivalrous noblemen — like the slender swords and scimitars of Toledo or Damascus or, of more recent fame, the swords of the Japanese Samurai. When the upper ranks of commoners began to share in the prerogatives and responsibilities of government in war and peace, the advance was rapid from spears and arrows to guns of all sorts. Surely it was the advance from aristocracy toward bourgeois middle-class democracy, says Hegel, that prompted human intelligence to invent the gun (the rifle and the equalizing pistol as well as the cannon), so that the privately personal forms of aristocratic bravery could begin to give way to the essentially impersonal forms of democratic bravery. The warheads that such missiles as these can carry are plainly the greatest democratic equalizers of all.

NIXON AND BREZHNEV TOASTING THE FUTURE

SOVIET ICBM IN MOSCOW'S RED SQUARE

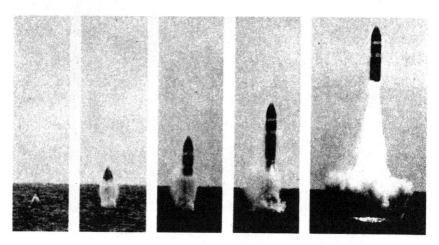

U.S. POSEIDON SUBMARINE-LAUNCHED MISSILE

Once only a President of the United States like George Washington could be first in assuming the risks of war as well as first in peace. Now that every adult person can claim equal rank in the prerogatives of peace, so must each and all of us together assume equally the risks of the common defense. From Excalibur to the multi-megaton warheads of the largest Soviet and American missiles: that has been the weaponry measure of the march of freedom. Abolish the democratic equalizers, return to swords, and serfdom will surely reappear once more, and perhaps slavery too, which still exists today, as we know, where weapons are truly primitive.

Can we disarm as some think and be free? Since 1961, many of our top presidential advisors coming out of the elite universities have insisted that we can. A few have even suggested that freedom is no longer something to be preferred to peace, when the price to be paid for it might mount as high as nuclear war. But in a speech titled "Preserving Our National Security," delivered at Winston-Salem, North Carolina, on March 16, 1978, President Nixon (then apparently getting another kind of advice from Harvard and Columbia) put the question in realistic perspective with these words:

> For most of human history, people have wished vainly that freedom — and the flowering of the human spirit that freedom nourishes — did not finally have to depend on force of arms. We, like our forebears, live in a time when those who would destroy liberty are restrained less by their respect for freedom than by their knowledge that those of us who cherish freedom are strong. We are a great nation made up of talented people. We can readily ... understand the basic lesson of history: that we need to be resolute and able to protect ourselves, to prevent threats and domination by others. No matter how peaceful and secure and easy the circumstances of our lives now seem, we have no guarantee that the blessings will endure. That is why we will always maintain

the strength which, God willing, we shall never need to use.

Those words echo the spirit of the political theoreticians and practical statesmen who drafted the American Declaration of Independence and later drew up the Federal Constitution. In the Declaration of Independence they assumed for us a "separate and equal station" among the powers of the earth; and in the Preamble to the Constitution, they charged us to form a more perfect national union, with an ever-expanding equality in freedom, for ourselves and our posterity. That is the direction along which our past — a legacy of freedom traceable back to the ancient Greeks and Jews through European and Roman Christendom — presses us into the future.

Tomorrow: A World-System of Free Nations

In our individual relations as moral beings, the commandment of our legacy of freedom states quite categorically: Be a free person and respect others as free persons, entitled to all the rights and charged with all the responsibilities that make up personality. In the sphere of international relations, the rule for us as a united people is the same: Be a sovereignly free nation and respect all other peoples as sovereignly free, with all the rights and responsibilities that make up free nationhood in a world of marvelously varied ethnic, political, religious, and cultural diversity.

It is after all, as Hegel says, in art, religion, and philosophy — not in economics or politics — that mankind raises itself in some measure above the destructive force of history. Economic systems come and go, and so, in time, do even the best-ordained of political constitutions. But art, with its time-arresting beauty, religion, with its supreme good of God-inspired love, and philosophy, with its wisdom or truth in which the beauty and goodness of art and religion are integrated, do not belong to time.

The beauty, goodness, and truth of these absolute moments of spirit, as Hegel calls them, are of universal value, to be shared by all who can appreciate them, regardless of race, creed, or ethnic origin. Still, it is through the politically-organized labors of nations that all three have their historical development. That is why those of us who are not alien-minded, who love our philosophic, religious, and artistic national heritages, must not let ourselves be intimidated — whether by ambitious despots or fearful cosmopolitans — into denying what we love. We must dare to be free; for, as Hegel says, freedom is the absolute goal of history. Its advance, as we have seen, has been slow. But we have now arrived at the point where the demand for it is global. Once, only the rare despot, ruling millions, had a sense of what it means to be free; then it became the turn of aristocratic elites; but now, as Hegel foresaw, freedom has at last become a possibility, and is rapidly becoming an actuality, for *all*, even for the traditionally enslavable peoples of the world.

Aristotle long ago taught that genuine political freedom is really nothing more than a united willingness of free men and women to fight and die rather than suffer enslavement. When such a willingness is absent, despots rule, whether armed with clubs or nuclear weapons. But when it is effectively organized, such a willingness is a most formidable instrument for the pursuit of happiness in this life. The nations that have such an organized willingness to die do not die, and neither are they enslaved; they make history instead. And out of their histories come the treasures of the world's high art, religion, and philosophy. For that reason we must boldly take our stand with the Solzhenitsyns and Abba Ebans of our time, as well as with Hegel, in reaffirming this historically validated truth: that the future of the world, if it is to have a civilized future, must belong to the diversity of sovereignly-free nations, large and small, and not to the uniformity of any global system of cultural nihilism, whether of the left or right.

IV. THE POLITICAL THOUGHT
OF G. W. F. HEGEL

To the question "what is truth?" Hegel replies (with Socrates and Aristotle and most other systematic thinkers of the West) that it is a ratio. He holds that it is not simple but composed, and that, in the pursuit of knowledge, it comes not among the first things, but among the last. More precisely: truth for Hegel is neither a subjective idea in itself nor an objective thing in itself, neither a universal abstractly conceived nor a particular empirically apprehended, but an adequate linking-together in reason (ratio) of thought and thing, universal and particular.

The entire Hegelian system as we have it in the *Encyclopedia of the Philosophical Sciences* is unmistakably an analytical exposition of truth as a ratio. Its three major parts develop the truth of idea as *idea in itself* (Science of Logic), the truth of thing as *idea in its otherness* (Philosophy of Nature), and the truth of the adequation of idea and thing *as idea come back to itself out of that otherness* (Philosophy of Mind).[1] Each of the parts, in turn, mirrors the structure of the whole; and so do the parts of the parts, down to the simplest constituent propositions, for every proposition or sentence capable of expressing even a modicum of truth is, according to Hegel, a linking together of subject and predicate, of particular and universal, of thought and thing.

The sciences that especially concern us here — the social, political, and historical sciences — are parts of a part of the Philosophy of Mind which, like the other two major divisions and the system as a whole, presents its contents first as idea (Subjective Mind), then as thing (Objective Mind), and finally as an adequate linking-together of idea and thing (Absolute Mind). The conclusion is hardly to be avoided, therefore, that in the least parts as well as in the whole of his system, Hegel quite deliberately sustains the classical definition of truth which, in its Latin form, survived into modern times as a commonplace of medieval philosophy: *veritas est adaequatio intellectus et res.*

Immanuel Kant, it is important to recall, had rejected that traditional notion of truth. Or rather, in his celebrated *Critique of Pure Reason*, he had begun by granting it, but only to dismiss it at once as something trivial. And Hegel criticizes him for it, particularly in the *Science of Logic* , where he defends the medieval commonplace as "a definition which is of great, and even of the highest value." Against Kant, he there argues that if the old notion of truth

is recalled in connection with the fundamental assertion of transcendental idealism, namely, that cognition by means of reason is not capable of apprehending the things-in-themselves, and that reality lies utterly outside the Notion [Begriff], then it is clear immediately that such a reason, which cannot establish a correspondence between itself and its object (the things-in-themselves), is an untrue idea; and equally untrue are things-in-themselves which do not correspond with the Notion of reason, a Notion which does not correspond with reality, and a reality which does not correspond with the Notion. If Kant had kept the idea of an intuitive understanding close to this definition of truth, then he would not have treated this idea, which expresses the required correspondence, as a figment of thought, but as truth.[2]

Because he adhered to an untrue idea of what truth is, Kant was foredoomed to fail in his attempt to assess the capacity of human reason to arrive at truth. Hegel characterized as a "mark of the diseased state of the age," the general adoption of the "despairing creed that our knowledge is only subjective." The natural belief of ordinary men in all ages gives the lie to such a view. Rightly understood, truth is objective; rightly understood, thought coincides with thing. Hegel cites Dante's insistence (*Paradiso* iv, 124-30) that the human intellect is certainly capable of attaining truth, and that, indeed, nothing short of truth can satisfy it. The business of philosophy, he concludes against Kant, is precisely to confirm the old belief that it is "the characteristic right of mind to know the truth" and thus "to bring into explicit consciousness what the world in all ages had believed."[3]

In his *Science of Logic*, Hegel refers us specifically to his *Phenomenology of Mind* for a detailed analysis of the limitations of Kant's approach to the question of knowledge. Kant's basic defect, according to Hegel, was that he "neither considered nor investigated the truly speculative ideas of the older philosophers about the notion of Mind," taking his departure in this area exclusively from Hume's skeptical treatment of the rationalist metaphysical doctrine of the mind. In his *Phenomenology* of 1806, Hegel assumed that same vantage point, accepting the Humean and Kantian formulations of the problem of truth; but then he went on to rectify the Kantian errors, giving us a vivid account of the riot of thought through which the mind, driven by doubt, must pass in rising to the level of "insight into what knowing really is."[4]

Of the *Phenomenology of Mind* it has been correctly said that it is the germination of a living seed which absorbs and consumes its environment in preparation for its own systematic growth, which is yet to come. In the process of getting to know what knowing really is, the mind initially takes for granted "the existence of the concrete formations of consciousness, such as individual and social morality, art and religion." But to arrive at its goal, it must free itself of all that it has received or absorbed uncritically. Thus — Hegel explains in retrospect — the development of consciousness traced in the *Phenomenology* involves a sort of cultural unraveling "of the matter or of the objects properly discussed in the special branches of philosophy." What belongs in the ratio of truth of the complete system is "prematurely dragged into the introduction," and that makes the exposition intricate.[5]

Practically all the distinguishable sciences of the three parts of the *Encyclopedia* make an appearance of sorts in the *Phenomenology of Mind* — but not in the form of truth. Their vast cultural wealth is poured into the consciousness of the individual mind to nourish it the way food nourishes the individual body. Just as the body in its growth from the fertilized egg recapitulates the great chain of animal forms that are implicit in its nature, so the mind of the individual recapitulates the experience of the family, civil society, state, and period of history into which it is born. Through self-criticism, conscious Mind, which is initially a captive of its cultural environment, must emerge, finally, as Free Mind, ready for the logic of truth in its systematic form. There is no avoiding that preliminary illogical, almost riotous confrontation with the fullness of human culture, however; for a large part of the task of preparing the mind for genuinely philosophic science is precisely to unravel the complexities of existential experience, and thus "to show how the questions men have usually raised about the nature of Knowledge, Faith, and the like — questions which they imagine to have no connection with abstract thoughts — are really reducible to the simple categories which first get cleared up in Logic."[6]

The *Phenomenology of Mind* is not to be confounded, therefore, with the system of the *Encyclopedia*. The former is an existential treatise in the modern sense. Whoever takes up the question of knowledge as posed by Hume and Kant and their disciples in our own time is certain to find himself at one turn or another of the path of the *Phenomenology* — which is a preparatory work of Conscious Mind. The *Encyclopedia*, on the other hand, is the consummate work of Free Mind. It presupposes that Conscious Mind has become Free through insight into what philosophic truth really is: an *adaequatio intellectus et res*, developed into a universal whole, each part of which consists of a ratio of ratios, analyzable downward in its rational necessity to the least meaningful linking-together of the basic parts of speech.

The Hegelian-Aristotelian Perspective

Because the truth of the Hegelian system is the whole in its organic articulation, there can be no specially favored beginning, no basic introductory science so completely true in itself that it must stand first. The notion of a beginning in philosophy has meaning, Hegel writes, "only in relation to a person who proposes to commence the study, and not in relation to science as science."[7] The system in its truth is a great "circle of education" without beginning and without end — a circle that freely turns upon itself, carrying its constituent sciences around with it, each in its distinctive place, fixed there by a rational necessity, each offering a distinctive approach (neither more nor less valid than any other) to the truth of the whole.

Only Free Mind can know the whole truth in its freedom; yet, paradoxically, it is only through knowledge of the truth that Mind is made free. As often as he discusses what true knowledge is and what results from reason's absorption in it, Hegel confronts this paradox. Repeatedly, he cites the Biblical admonition: "You shall know the truth and the truth shall make you free." And almost invariably, he couples with it Spinoza's paradoxical formulation of the ancient truth that freedom is "insight into necessity." Hegel thus sums it all up in the opening pages of his *Encyclopedia*:

> Truth is only possible as a universe or totality of thought; and the freedom of the whole, as well as the necessity of the several sub-divisions, which it implies, are only possible when these are discriminated and defined. . . . Each of the parts of philosophy is a philosophical whole, a circle rounded and complete in itself. In each of these

parts, however, the philosophical idea is found in a particular specificality or medium. The single circle, because it is a real totality, bursts through the limits imposed by its special medium, and gives rise to a wider circle. The whole of philosophy in this way resembles a circle of circles. The idea appears in each circle, but, at the same time, the whole idea is constituted by the system of these particular phases, and each is a necessary member of the organization.[8]

Like the satellite epicycles of the ancient and modern astronomies, each science of the system of sciences has a separate center of its own and a relatively independent progression of its own around that center. The ultimate moving principle is that of the whole; but that is by no means an exclusive or restrictive principle. On the contrary, as Hegel writes, "genuine philosophy makes it a principle to sustain every particular principle."[9] Indeed, because its organic connection with the whole leaves it relatively free in its self-centered progression, every one of the specialized disciplines of the *Encyclopedia* has a tendency to "burst through" the limits of its special medium and extend its sway at the expense of its neighbors. The science of history, for instance, has always had an insatiable appetite for devouring neighboring disciplines, claiming that its sweep ought to encompass all that is humanly known or knowable. Similar claims have been advanced more recently by political science, sociology, economics, psychology, anthropology, and even bio-chemistry. Obviously it is only the systematic discipline of the whole, however arrived at, that can by rational necessity keep the constituent disciplines in place.

The organic conception here is far removed from the Kantian critical perspective. The premises of transcendental idealism with respect to the nature of mind and truth are abandoned in favor of the dialectical realism of Aristotle. Of this there can be no serious doubt. The staggeringly humble tribute to Aristotelian thought in the concluding lines of the *Encyclopedia*, where Hegel expresses his own loftiest thought in Aristotle's Greek, is well known. What needs to be stressed here is that the Hegelian system in its entirety — as distinct from the introductory *Phenomenology of Mind* — is essentially Aristotelian from its immediate approach to the question of knowledge to its full exposition of truth as Absolute Mind.

In his *History of Philosophy*, Hegel credits Aristotle with the initial logical insight into what knowing really is, praising him especially for the clarity of his distinctions in remarking how, even in its most abstract expression, truth is not something simple but a ratio. Aristotle had emphasized in his *De Interpretatione* (which is essentially a grammar of logic), that subjects and predicates and linking verbs, ''as isolated terms, are not yet either true or false,'' for "truth and falsity imply combination and separation." Of the process of combination in thought, Aristotle had said further (in a very "Hegelian" vein): "Neither are 'to be' and 'not to be' and the participle 'being' significant of any truth, unless something is added, but imply a copulation, of which we cannot form a conception apart from the things coupled."[10]

It is on the insight so abstractly expressed here that Hegel constructs his grand "cycle of education." Ultimately, the "things coupled" in his *Encyclopedia* are all the constituent truths of all traditional disciplines of scientific knowledge, ranging from the abstract sciences of logic and mathematics, through the mechanical, physical, and organic branches of natural science, to the cycle of man-centered studies that culminate in the sciences of artistic making, religious behavior, and God-centered metaphysical speculation. Just as in the mathematical sciences, the goal is a formulation of truth as a set of mathematical ratios, so in the all-comprehending system of sciences, the goal is an all-comprehending philosophical ratio of ratios. Though he did not attain it himself, Aristotle had projected just such a goal for philosophy; and to realize it has been, according to Hegel, the proper task of philosophy ever since. Hegel is thus characterizing his own philosophic labors of a lifetime, as well as the limits of Aristotle's achievement, when he remarks in the *History of Philosophy* that

> the whole of Aristotle's philosophy really requires recasting, so that all his determinations can be brought into a necessary systematic whole — not a systematic whole which is correctly divided into its parts, and in which no part is forgotten, all being set forth in their proper order, but one in which there is one living organic whole, in which each part is held to be a part, and the whole alone as such is true. Aristotle, in the *Politics*, for instance, often gives expression to this truth.[11]

That his *Encyclopedia* is offered as a recasting of the Aristotelian philosophy, Hegel himself assures us quite explicitly in many places, and perhaps most explicitly in his introduction to the *Philosophy of Mind*. There he says that "the books of Aristotle's *De Anima*, along with his discussions on the *psyche*'s special aspects and states [discussions pursued in the *Nichomachean Ethics, Politics, Rhetoric, Poetics, Metaphysics*, and related writings] are still by far the most admirable, perhaps even the sole work of philosophical value on this topic." And his conclusion is that "the main aim of a philosophy of mind can only be to re-introduce unity of idea and principle into the theory of mind, and so reinterpret the lesson of those Aristotelian books."[12]

Following Aristotle's lead, Hegel distinguishes three developmental phases, or functional aspects of Mind, to which the designations Subjective, Objective, and Absolute correspond. In its subjective development, Mind acts to rationalize, or assimilate to its own nature, an animal actuality which is only potentially human. The Aristotelian leads for this phase are clearly indicated in the *De Anima*. In its objective development (and here Hegel follows closely the leads of the *Ethics* and *Politics*), Mind shapes for itself the rational, or *mindful* realities of family-life, civil society, and states, whose coming into being and passing away constitutes the course of history. Finally, in its absolute development (corresponding to the sphere of Aristotle's *Metaphysics*, Book X of the *Ethics*, the *Poetics*, and related passages of the *De Anima*), Mind transcends objective history, arresting time in the aesthesis of inspired art, overcoming mortality in the ecstasis of revealed religion, and assimilating itself to God (*nóesis nóeseos nóesis* — thought thinking thought) in the experience of *sophia*, where the highest intuitive and discursive reasoning — the *nous* and *episteme* of Aristotle — are one.

It is important to keep in mind the essentially Aristotelian perspective in all of this, so that we may guard ourselves against the error of students of Hegel who don't know Aristotle and who insist on approaching the Hegelian system through Marx or contemporary existentialism: the error of imagining that Hegel is straying off on some needlessly obscure, tortuous new path of epistemological speculation, spurred on by his apparent mania for triads, at precisely those turns of his exposition where he means to be most respectful of the Aristotelian tradition.

The Sciences of Objective Mind

Within this broad Aristotelian design, Hegel distinguishes almost all the "disciplines" that have traditionally enjoyed academic status as sciences of human nature and conduct, and several that have acquired such status since his time. For most of the minor sciences, the definitions are necessarily brief in the *Encyclopedia*, in keeping with its character as a handbook; but many cursorily treated there are considered at length, with particularized discussions of methods of study and scientific validation, in the *Philosophy of Right*, *Philosophy of History*, *Philosophy of Fine Art*, *Philosophy of Religion*, and *History of Philosophy*, all of which are elaborations of the Philosophy of Mind.

From the standpoint of classification in the social or behavioral sciences, Hegel's broad distinctions of Subjective, Objective, and Absolute are very instructive. In his day they might have served, as he said, to re-introduce "unity of idea and principle" to a field where speculative chaos reigned. And one ventures to suggest that a general acceptance of them now might greatly facilitate the task of the many hard-pressed academicians who are today charged with regulating the seemingly endless, overlapping, proliferation of specialized disciplines in the field.

The sciences of society, politics, and history, strictly defined, make up the cycle of Objective Mind. But as they presuppose the "results" of the preceding sciences of Subjective Mind, it will be necessary, by way of introduction, to review cursorily the matter and form of those sciences.

Under Subjective Mind, Hegel distinguishes the sciences of anthropology, phenomenology, and psychology — all of which today qualify, on some one or another of the modern listings, as social or behavioral sciences. Anthropology is defined, in accordance with its etymological meaning, as the most general of the sciences of man. It focuses on the least common denominator of manhood: on the very *idea* — as Plato would say — of *anthropos*; or rather, in Aristotelian terms, on the characteristic act of manhood, through which the physical, self nutritional, sentient, passionate, and emotional activities of an animal existence are "humanized."

The systematic science of phenomenology (not to be confounded with the "voyage of discovery" which prepares the mind for true science), presupposes the humanizing activities studied in anthropology. On its higher level, phenomenology traces the activities of Mind that transform animal awareness into thoroughly human consciousness, then into self-consciousness, and finally into that doubling, or "mirroring" of self-consciousness which Hegel calls Reason (*Vernunft*) in full potency, as distinguished from the mere Understanding (*Verstand*) of consciousness and self-consciousness.

Psychology takes up the activity of Subjective Mind where phenomenology leaves off, tracing its development, through self-analysis, on the levels of theoretic and practical reason, to the level of potentially productive, or *willful* reason. As in the Freudian psychological self-analysis, so in the Hegelian, what emerges is the perfection of Subjective Mind as "Free Mind" — as mind become master in its own house (to use the renowned Freudian expression) and able, therefore, to overcome its subjectivity.

Anthropology, phenomenology, and psychology, thus defined, are introspective sciences of man. There are no objective "phenomena," no "evidences of things seen" to be "saved" by them. For validation of their measure of truth, scientists specializing in such fields must rely ultimately on subjective insight. In this respect, their relationship to the sciences of Objective Mind that immediately follow parallels the relationship of the Science of Logic to the Philosophy of Nature in the system as a whole.

Like the sciences of mechanics, physics, and organics that make up the Philosophy of Nature, the sciences of Objective Mind are objective in the strict sense. In both spheres the method of scientific study is therefore essentially the same. There are, on the one hand, external phenomena which must be taken for granted as empirically given, and, on the other, principles of thought, or organizing ideas, elaborated as hypotheses, that are not empirically given. The external phenomena are the "things," the hypotheses are the "thoughts" that must be adequately "linked-together," in reason, if the sciences of Objective Mind or those of the Philosophy of Nature are to have a valid ratio of truth in them.

It is, indeed, only the specific content or subject matter of the sciences of Objective Mind that distinguishes them from the natural sciences, in Hegel's scheme. Instead of testing the adequacy of their generalizing notions or hypotheses through direct observation of the characteristic motions of empirical phenomena on the level of me-

chanics, physics, and organics, they do so through direct
observation of the phenomena of man, as he actually lives
now, or has lived in the past, in family, civic, and political
association with his fellows.

Again and again, in the *Philosophy of Right* and the
Philosophy of History (which together cover the same ground
as the section on Objective Mind in the *Encyclopedia*),
Hegel reminds us of the obvious fact that the evidences of
man's present and past existence as a social being have an
objective authority for our consciousness at least as com-
pelling as that of the "sun, moon, mountains, rivers, and
the natural objects of all kinds by which we are surrounded."[13] Indeed, he insists that, since the aim of empirical science is to trace the operation of rational laws in the
phenomena under study, the social sciences are specially
favored in this respect. For it is the rational activity of man
— the practical and productive reasoning of his Free Mind
— that fashions the human institutions and institutional
histories that are the proper objects of study in the theo-
retical sciences of Objective Mind. As Hegel explains in the
Preface to the *Philosophy of Right*:

> So far as nature is concerned, people grant that it is
> nature as it is which philosophy has to bring within its
> ken . . . that nature is inherently rational, and that what
> knowledge has to investigate and grasp in concepts is this
> actual reason present in it; not the formations and
> accidents evident to the superficial observer, but nature's
> eternal harmony, in the sense of the law and essence
> immanent within it. The ethical world, on the other hand
> [the world of family, civil society, statehood, and his-
> tory], is somehow not authorized (according to the bias
> of some) to enjoy the good fortune which springs from
> the fact that it is reason itself which has achieved power
> and mastery within that element and which maintains
> and has its home there. [While nature is assumed to be
> immanently rational] the universe of objective mind is
> thus supposed rather to be left to the mercy of chance
> and caprice, to be God-forsaken; and the result, from

this standpoint, is that if the ethical world is Godless, truth lies outside it, and at the same time, since even so reason is supposed to be in it as well, truth becomes nothing but a problem.[14]

Hegel very emphatically denies the view that the natural sciences — and particularly the mathematical sciences of celestial and terrestrial mechanics (astronomy and physics) — ought to be regarded as the sciences *par excellence* upon which all other sciences, and particularly the social sciences, ought eventually to pattern themselves. His arguments against such an assumption illuminate the seeming paradox of the fact that, when Sir Francis Bacon proclaimed a new beginning for natural science in the 17th century, he took his cue (as he acknowledges) from the founder of modem political science: Machiavelli. What Machiavelli had so successfully done with the science of politics, Bacon argued, ought to serve as a model for what obviously needed to be done for the advancement of a long-stagnated natural science. With profound insight into the making of states, Machiavelli had undertaken to trace the *laws of statecraft* as statecraft really is, rather than as, according to the moralists, it *ought to be*.

How can natural scientists apply Machiavelli's example in their field? How can the method of Machiavelli's political science be made to stand as a model for chemists and physicists? Bacon's brilliant suggestion is that chemists and physicists should hereafter apply themselves to the study of empirical phenomena that are, like states, man-made — phenomena to be produced by a *craft* which is of the same order, though on a much more primitive level, as Machiavelli's *state craft*. That Baconian *craft*, through which natural science might hope to match Machiavelli's political science, is, of course, the craft of experimentation. Needless to say, scientific experiments as Bacon conceived them are man-made. And precisely because they are man-made, with human reason built into their minutest detail, study of them to ascertain their laws is much more rewarding than the study of empirical phenomena that are not man-made. Experimental science — the glory of the modern world — is thus, from Hegel's point of view, a very specialized part of the social or behavioral sciences: a specialized part that is accurate in its results, from a logical mathematical point of view, to the measure of its relative emptiness. An experiment with a lever in a laboratory, for instance, is man-made in the same sense that the new state of Israel is man-made. And it is no doubt true that a Ben Gurion, who has actually experimented with the making of states, is probably much better able to comprehend the truth of the science of politics as Hegel expounds it, than the average experimenter with levers, who fails to recognize the *social* nature of experimental science, is able to comprehend the truth of the science of mechanics.

Giambattista Vico had of course made the same point in his *Scienza Nuova*. What mankind has itself made men can know better than they can know the natural things that God, or chance, has made. And this is true, for Hegel as for Vico, ranging upward from the least artifacts of primitive peoples, through all the utilitarian products that serve human ends in civil society, to all the things of fine art, religious worship, and high philosophy that constitute the grandeur of history's great states, empires, and world civilizations.

The same Free Mind of man that "makes" a controlled experiment in a physics laboratory has, needless to say, also made the laboratory itself, as well as the " Advanced Institute" of higher learning that envelops it, and the surrounding college town, civil society, and political order apart from which the pursuit of science is an impossibility. Free Mind is, as we noted, the perfection of Subjective Mind, or Mind which, through psychological self-analysis, has overcome its subjectivity and is able, therefore, to objectify, or make actual, what it implicitly is.

Free Mind first manifests itself objectively, writes Hegel, through the assertion of a universal, willful claim on all it surveys; and the disciplined study of that characteristic act of Mind as Will is distinguished by Hegel as the science of Abstract Right, or theory of Law — first of the philosophical sciences of Objective Mind. In asserting its willful claim on everything, Free Mind acts as if it knew no bounds — as if it had actually heard the God of *Genesis* say to it: "Be fruitful, and multiply, and replenish the earth, and subdue it: and have dominion over the fish of the sea, and over the fowl of the air, and over every living thing that moveth upon the earth." But, as in *Genesis*, so in the Hegelian system, Free Mind, in solitary possession of but a single body, finds that it cannot go it alone objectively. In attempting to exercise its claim on all things, it is again and again frustrated and forced, eventually, to seek a compensatory satisfaction in self-righteous, moral alienation from the objective world. The science that focuses on this retreat of Free Mind back into itself is the science of Morality.

Together, Hegel's sciences of Abstract Right and Morality give us an updated recasting of Aristotle's *Ethics*, the conclusion of which is that the individual as person and moral subject cannot realize his individual ends in isolation. Only lately have Right and Morality come into their own as objects of lively if not yet disciplined study in the modern curriculum of the social sciences. But in America, at any rate, they have come in with a vengeance, on the heels of the Negro Civil-Rights movement. It is a matter of newspaper headlines that, after years of fiercely asserting an abstract personal right, the American Negro has experienced an objective frustration that has constrained him to seek a compensatory satisfaction in self-righteous, moral alienation from the objective world. Negroes and the social scientists who study their moral frustration have had to learn the hard way — which is to say, empirically — the ancient truth that Free Mind, whether in a black or a white body, has a better chance of realizing its ends in the objective world if it enters it as a family member.

The "results" of Free Mind's experience in Abstract

Right and Morality are the notions of right and wrong, of good and bad, of what ought and ought not to be. And these results are the presuppositions of the further development of the sciences of Objective Mind which are outlined in the *Encyclopedia* and elaborated in the *Philosophy of Right* under the headings Family, Civil Society, and State. These sciences, which are "social" in the strict sense, provide us with what is unquestionably an updated, Aristotelian *Politics*. Man, Aristotle had tried to demonstrate, is by nature — not by convention — a political animal. And his capacity to speak is perhaps the most distinctive sign of his political nature, in that, while mere voice (such as many animals possess) suffices to indicate pain and pleasure, it requires speech to "indicate the advantageous and the harmful, and therefore also the right and wrong."[15] In words that express Hegel's view as well, Aristotle had thus marked, in this respect, the transition from ethics to politics:

> For it is the special property of man in distinction from the other animals that he alone has perception of good and bad and right and wrong and the other moral qualities, and it is partnership in these things that makes up the family unit or household and the state.[16]

As in Aristotle, so in Hegel, politics in its broadest sense, as distinguished from the personal ethics and subjective morality of the individual, begins with *economia* — the science of the family unit. From a cultural standpoint, it is regrettable that modern derivatives of the ancient Greek word have not retained its original significance. Our English word "economics," for instance, hardly serves any longer to give us an adequate idea of the original thing. A new content has crept in, gradually crowding out the old, which is now left to fend for itself academically, without benefit of a scientific-sounding name. To identify precisely what he means, and thus avoid cultural confusion, Hegel uses the prosaic designation "die Familie"; but it should be noted that in so doing he is, in effect, following the

example of the learned I5th century humanist Leon Battist'
Alberti who, in reviving the ancient study of *economia* as
Xenophon had perfected it, called his book simply *Della
Famiglia.*

In Marriage — first of the three moments of family
life distinguished by Hegel — the "I-thou" personal relationship of man and woman, drawn together to perpetuate
the species, becomes a "we" relationship with a distinct
personality of its own. That "we" is strengthened in its
unity through external embodiment in a Family Capital —
second moment of the notion — which is not "yours and
mine" but "ours." But full objectivization of the bond that
unites husband and wife comes only with realization of the
third moment — the generation and rearing of children, "in
whom the parents can see objectified the entirety of their
union. . . . For, while in their goods, their unity is embodied
only in an external thing, in their children it is embodied
in a spiritual one in which the parents are loved and which
they love."[17]

Under the rearing of children, Hegel gives us a brief
but very suggestive "science of education" which is further
developed in the discussions on Civil Society and the State.
As a function of the family, education has a negative as well
as a positive aspect. On the positive side, its object is to
instill ethical feelings that will enable the child "to live its
early years in love, trust, and obedience"; whereas, on its
negative side, its object is to raise the child out of its
original state of dependence "to self-subsistence and freedom of personality and so to the level where he has the
power to leave the natural unity of the family." Once
educated to freedom of personality (within the "we" experience of family life), the child claims recognition as a
person in his own right, and the unity of the original family
is on the point of dissolution — an inevitable dissolution
that becomes total in the death of the parents.[18]

Dissolution of the family, which may be gradual,
eventually leaves the surviving members on their own in

the network of "I-thou" relationships that make up Civil
Society. They move into Civil Society as individuals, but, if
they are products of well-ordered families, they already
have in themselves the "we" experience of true community.
They are ready in themselves, in other words, for the
organic partnership of marriage and the formation of
another family unit, at the same time that, as individuals,
they are competing and cooperating with their fellows for
the satisfaction of their personal needs. The experience of
voluntary cooperation in Civil Society coupled with the
experience of family membership prepares human beings,
finally, for fully-conscious participation in the "we" relationship of political community, upon which the objective
subsistence of family life and the civil relationships ultimately depend.

In a famous "*addition*" to the *Philosophy of Right*,
Hegel observes that Civil Society (*bürgerliche Gesellschaft*) is
a distinctly modern development, in the sense that "only in
the modern world have all the various elements or determinations of the idea received their due."[19] In this connection, Hegel notes that the ancient Greeks lived their lives
almost exclusively as family members and as citizens or
dependent subjects of a tightly regulated political community. Public law penetrated deeply into the privacy of
family life, leaving virtually no middle ground for a "private" individual or associational existence independent of
the characteristic ties of family and state. Separation from
the former resulted almost simultaneously in full absorption by the latter. From the point of view of Greek social
science, therefore, economics (in its original sense) and the
science of politics exhausted the field.

Only in the modern world have family and state
come to be separated, objectively, by a vast middle-ground
where many human beings born out of wedlock, or separated from their parents in childhood, can manage to live
their entire lives without conscious experience of membership in the social orders of family or state. For the ancients,

that middle ground was but an abstract, psychological moment of social alienation; whereas, in the modern world, it is precisely there that Objective Mind has fashioned for itself the complex life of Civil Society, which has, in turn, called into being an entire cycle of new sciences whose focus of interest is *more* than economic, in the ancient Greek sense, at the same time that it is also always *less* than political. Defining the limits of this distinctive associational achievement of the modern world, Hegel writes :

> Civil Society is the realm of difference that separates family and state, mediating between them, even though in point of time its formation comes after the state, which its own objective existence presupposes as a necessary condition . . . . If the state is represented to us as a unity of persons which is only a contractual arrangement or partnership, then what is really meant is only civil society. Unfortunately, many modern social theoreticians appear at present to be incapable of conceiving any other theory of the state than this.[20]

Cautioning readers against the tendency of his contemporaries to confound state and civil society, Hegel repeatedly stresses that the state no less than the family is an organic union; that its citizens as citizens are not in an "I-thou" relationship with one another, but, rather, like family members, they constitute a substantive "we" that they tend to love and value more than they value their individual existences. In Civil Society, on the contrary,

> each member is his own end and everything else is nothing to him. And yet, because each must of necessity enter into relationships with others to realize his ends, those others, who would otherwise be objects of indifference, become indispensable means. Through this utilitarian linkage with others, each member's particularized pursuit of a particular end is universalized, its satisfaction being attainable only in the simultaneous attainment of satisfaction by others. Because the particularity of interests that constitute it are thus inevitably univer-

> salized, the whole sphere of civil society becomes an
> arena of mediation of opposites, where there is free play
> for every idiosyncrasy, every talent, every accident of
> birth and fortune, and where waves of every passion gush
> forth, regulated only by reason [Objective Mind] glint-
> ing through them.[21]

Already in Hegel's time, the new science that traced the
characteristic acts of mind glinting through the intricate
web of human relations in civil society bore the compound
name of Political Economy [Staatsökonomie] — suggesting
a fusing, or even a confusing, of the traditional sciences of
family and state. Of Political Economy, Hegel writes:

> This is one of the sciences which have arisen out of the
> conditions of the modern world. Its development af-
> fords the interesting spectacle (as in Smith, Say, and
> Ricardo) of thought working upon the endless mass of
> details which confront it at the outset and extracting
> therefrom the simple principles of the thing, the Under-
> standing effective in the thing and directing it. It is
> gratifying to find, in the sphere of needs, this show of
> rationality lying in the thing and working itself out there;
> but if we look at it from the opposite point of view, this
> is the sphere in which the Understanding with its subjec-
> tive aims and moral fancies vents its discontents and
> moral frustration.[22]

It is in the competitive self-seeking of individuals in civil
society that the personal moral frustration considered in
depth by Hegel under the heading Morality actually takes
place — a frustration that is relieved, in fact, only through
entry into marriage or through the conscious assumption
of rights and responsibilities of citizenship. But, while
moral frustration is inextricably woven into the fabric of
Civil Society, the science that studies the complex web of
that fabric is nevertheless, in Hegel's judgment,

> a science that does honor to thought because it finds laws
> in a mass of accidents. It is fascinating to see how action
> is linked with action, and how such linked actions fall
> into groups, influence others, and are helped or hin-

dered by others . . . . It has a parallel in the science of planetary motions which, while always appearing complex and irregular to the eye, are nevertheless governed by ascertainable laws.[23]

Hegel expresses great admiration for the achievements of specialists in the "dismal" new science and is not surprised that, absorbed as they are in the excitements of studying a social creation of their own era, many of them should be inclined to ignore the social realities of family life and state that had absorbed the entire interest of their predecessors since the days of Plato and Aristotle. His concern is not to belittle the new discipline, but rather to guard its legitimacy, together with that of the traditional social sciences, by carefully distinguishing the characteristic acts of human association that are the primary object of study in each.

The paragraphs of Hegel's *Staatsökonomie* in which he outlines the "laws" of the internal dialectic of Civil Society have had a tremendous historical impact. His analysis of how that dialectic results in the formation of social classes and special interest groups that compete to universalize their interests fascinated Karl Marx. And, at the point where Marx's powers of concentration apparently failed — which is to say, where the dialectic of civil society results in the formation of "service" institutions for the regulation of civil rights, the "policing" of civil disorders, and for the ultimate resolution of internal conflicts through external expansion — it was Lenin's turn to be fascinated.

Surely worthy of comparison with the scientific achievement of a Kepler or Newton is the economy of thought with which Hegel was able to formulate the "law of social dialectic" in three pages of his *Philosophy of Right*. First he reviews the lessons of the English laissez-faire economists, noting how the untrammeled internal development of civil society results in an over-production of industrial goods and population, and thus in large-scale unemployment. Then he considers the social consequences

of such combined over-productivity and under-employ-
ment, observing that

> when the standard of living of a large mass of people falls
> below a certain subsistence level — a level regulated
> automatically as the one necessary for a member of the
> society — and when there is a consequent loss of the sense
> of right and wrong, of honesty and the self-respect which
> makes a man insist on maintaining himself by his own
> work and effort, the result is the creation of a rabble of
> paupers. At the same time this brings with it, at the other
> end of the social scale, conditions which greatly facilitate
> the concentration of disproportionate wealth in few
> hands.[24]

If the wealthier classes, or charitable foundations, attempt
by direct means to guarantee the old standard of living of
the unemployed, regardless of whether they work or not;
or if (despite the fact of over-production) make-work
schemes are introduced; the result — according to Hegel —
is the same: "The evil to be removed remains and is indeed
intensified by the very methods adopted to alleviate it. We
have thus the seeming paradox that, despite an excess of
wealth, civil society is not rich enough, i.e., its own resources are insufficient to check excessive poverty."[25]

In all the pages of *Das Kapital*, Marx succeeds in
adding nothing essential to Hegel's brief formulation.
And, as for the Hobson-Leninist extension of the Marxist
doctrine in the theory of capitalist imperialism, here is
Hegel's brief summation:

> The inner dialectic of civil society then drives it beyond
> its own shores to seek markets, and so the necessary
> means of subsistence, in other lands which either lack
> the means of which it has a superfluity, or are generally
> backward in industries . . . . The far-flung connecting-link
> of the sea affords the means for the colonizing activity —
> sporadic or systematic — to which the mature civil society
> is driven and by which it supplies to a part of its popula-
> tion a return to life on the family basis in a new land and

so also supplies itself with a new demand and field for its industry.[26]

Hegel, incidentally, insisted that all colonies founded by the modern European states would inevitably gain independence, and that their independence would prove to be "of the greatest advantage to the mother country, just as the emancipation of slaves turns out to the greatest advantage of the owners."[27]

It should be noted here that Marx and Lenin (though the latter in theory only) pursued the line of reasoning of Hegel's contemporaries who confounded civil society and the state. For Marx, the only social reality in the modern world was civil society. The development of capitalism, he held, had reduced the old institutions of family and state to the status of instruments, or tools, for the selfish satisfaction of individual, group, or class interests in the competitions of civil society.

But Hegel had analyzed that "new economic" view of modern society long before it was explicitly advanced by the authors of the *Communist Manifesto* as a revolutionary revelation; and he had rejected it, even as he rejected by anticipation, the related view of John Dewey, and Arthur F. Bentley which now prevails in the American academy: the view that the patterned activities of classes, interest groups, and "service" institutions in civil society are the sole characteristically political activities, and that political science therefore wastes its time when it looks beyond interest groups, etc., for a higher form of political reality.

In Hegel's judgment, all such Marxist or "systems-analysis" views of society illustrate the error of what has lately come to be called scientific "reductionism." Aristotle had written against such reductionism as applied to politics in the opening pages of his treatise on the subject, where he said that those who insisted that a political community differed only quantitatively from other forms of human association were wrong. Hegel, in fact, explicitly supports Aristotle's polemical demonstration that *politeia* is not an extended family, or an elaborated employer-employee relationship, and certainly not a master-slave or exploiter-exploited class relationship; that it is on the contrary a qualitatively distinct community of free and equal human beings united in pursuit of the highest conceivable earthly ends of free men.

In strictly Hegelian terms, *politeia* is the objective reality Free Mind must fashion for itself if it is to realize all its potentialities — potentialities that cannot be realized in any associations, however large or small, of family-members as such, or civil-society burghers as such, but only in a more perfect union, or *we* relationship, of free and equal citizens.

Hegel thus accepts literally Aristotle's definition of *politeia* as the "government of men free and equal" and of political science as the science of such government.[28] He departs from Aristotle only to deny (but it is a very large *only*) that any human beings are by nature, rather than voluntarily, slaves. He affirms, on the contrary, that, through the extension of Christianity and the development of civil society, it is now possible for all human beings, including emancipated slaves and their descendents, to be educated up to equality in freedom; if not perfectly, as individuals, at least in the form of that politically shared willingness to die rather than endure enslavement, which characterizes the free life of sovereign states, large or small, in the modern world.

But how do the burghers of civil society overcome the tendency of its internal dialectic to "polarize" them into a rich few and a pauperized many? How is the so-called inevitable contradiction of modern capitalist society to be intentionally resolved so as to make a more perfect political union come into being instead? Hegel's answer is: through voluntary association in what he identifies as the "corporations" of civil society. By corporations, Hegel means every possible voluntary association of producers of goods and services, whether on the ownership, management, or wage-earning level. Here is the part of the Hegelian social and political theory that fascinated Benedetto Croce and Giovanni Gentile. It was a theory resembling Hegel's notion of a "corporation" society, to serve as the basis of a "corporate" state, that those philosophers advanced as an answer to the Marxist-Leninist, anti-political, revolutionary doctrine. But far more faithful to the Hegelian view in this respect (precisely because of its emphasis on the satisfaction of the individual in the resultant political community) is the corporate ideal of Herbert Croly's *Promise of American Life.*

The terms in which Croly argues for the continued "combination of capital," to be accompanied by "completer unionization" of labor, and the development of a "responsible concentration" of political power in government, "in order to maintain the balance," is strictly Hegelian, in form as well as content. And that Croly thesis, which so greatly influenced Theodore Roosevelt, is perhaps most Hegelian where its author concludes: "An organic unity binds the three aspects of the system together; and in so far as a constructive tendency becomes powerful in any one region, it will tend by its own force to introduce constructive methods of organization into the other divisions of the economic, political and social body."[29]

In explaining how membership in business corporations, labor unions, and governmental agencies prepares burghers for integration in the free life of political community, Hegel observes that it is only in the absence of such associations that the polarization of society into a minority of rich capitalists and a majority of pauperized, unemployed workers can occur. "Unless he is a member of a corporation," Hegel writes,

> an individual is without rank or dignity, his isolation reduces his productive activity to mere self-seeking . . . . We saw earlier that in fending for himself a member of civil society is also working for others. But this unconscious compulsion is not enough; it is in the Corporation

that it first changes into a conscious and thoughtful ethical mode of life. Of course corporations must fall under the higher surveillance of the state, because otherwise they would ossify, build themselves in, and decline into a miserable system of castes. In and by itself, however, a corporation is not a closed caste; its purpose is rather to bring an isolated trade into the social order and elevate it to a sphere in which it gains strength and respect.[30]

The corporation thus becomes for its members a kind of family; and Hegel, in fact, concludes his discussion of Civil Society with the observation that "as the family was the first, so the corporation is the second ethical root of the state," the two serving as the only securely fixed points "round which the unorganized atoms of civil society revolve."

Yet it would be completely erroneous to assume that political community, or the state in its proper sense, develops out of the dialectic of civil society. "Actually," Hegel writes, "the state as such is not so much the result as the beginning. It is within the state that the family is first developed into civil society, and it is the Idea of the state itself which disrupts itself into the two moments" out of which, by scientific analysis, we seem to "deduce" its existence.[31]

By the time the state in its actuality is made the object of study in Hegel's *Philosophy of Right,* it is clear that the method of exposition to that point has been strictly Aristotelian. The whole has been analyzed into its constituent elements so that the organic connection and dependence of the parts on the whole may be displayed. Aristotle had said plainly enough that, while individual human beings form and perpetuate families and states through their common intercourse, the state is nevertheless, in the order of nature, prior to the family and the individual. In what is perhaps his most brilliant brief summary of the dialectic of the progression of sciences in this sphere,

Hegel distinguishes the several sciences according to their objects of study;

> We begin with something abstract, namely, with the Notion of Will; we then go on to the actualization of the as yet abstract will in an external existent, to the sphere of formal right; from there we go on to the will that is reflected into itself out of external existence, to the sphere of morality; and thirdly and lastly we come to the will that unites within itself these two abstract moments and is therefore the concrete, ethical will. In the ethical sphere itself we again start from an immediate, from the natural, undeveloped shape possessed by the ethical mind in the *family;* then we come to the *splitting up* of the ethical substance in *civil society;* and finally, in the State, attain the unity and truth of those two one-sided forms of the ethical mind. But this course followed by our exposition does not in the least mean that we would make the ethical life *later in time* than right and morality, or would explain the family and civil society to be *antecedent* to the State in the *actual* world. On the contrary, we are well aware that the ethical life is the foundation of right and morality, as also that the family and civil society with their well-ordered distinctions already presuppose the existence of the State. In the *philosophical* development of the ethical sphere, however, we cannot begin with the State, since in this the ethical sphere has unfolded itself into its most concrete form, whereas the beginning is necessarily something abstract. For this reason, the moral sphere, too, must be considered before the ethical sphere, although the former to a certain extent comes to view in the latter only as a sickness.[32]

Briefly put, one may say that *abstract right* with its positing of the will in external things, *morality* with its subjective justification, the ethical life of the *family* with its immediate bond of love, and *civil society* with its mediated bonds of need, are moments analyzable out of the actuality of the life of the *state.* The *persons* of abstract right, the *subjects* of morality and conscience, the *members* of families, and the *burghers* of civil society enter the life of the state as *citizens,* to constitute a new whole qualitatively different, as we have stressed, from all other human associations. As to what characteristically unites citizens in a true state, Hegel writes: "Liberty and equality are indeed the foundation of the state." But he hastens to add that they are the foundation which is ''as the most abstract, so also the most superficial, and for that reason the most familiar."[33]

The State is the perfection of Objective Mind in the same sense that Free Mind is the perfection of Subjective Mind. Free Mind overcomes the original subjectivity of mind through psychological self-analysis. Similarly, the State overcomes its absorption in the processes of civil society (where classes attempt to use its powers to advance class interests) by the self-constituting processes of rational law.

States have a constituted actuality that can be studied objectively. One can observe empirically how the constitution of one's own state — whether Athens, Sparta, or Rome, England, the United States, or China — actually functions from day to day. A comparative study of such constitutions — comparative "systems-analysis," we would call it today — leads to knowledge of the essential structure of a political community as such. But each state has, of course, an historical development of its own that can be studied in itself as well as comparatively. The Athenian constitution, for example, was originally a despotic rule of one man, but there took place a gradual devolution of power, through a dozen or more political crises, from the rule of one through the rule of few and then of many; whereas the Spartan constitution, with its carefully separated and balanced powers, hardly changes at all in a comparable interval of time. Systems-analysis and constitutional histories were the basis upon which Aristotle founded his *Politics* – but only after having reviewed the theories of politics advanced by his predecessors in the field. And

Hegel does the same. As T. M. Knox correctly remarks in his notes to the *Philosophy of Right,* according to Hegel,

> a study of positive law [systems-analysis] and history must precede the philosophy of right. The philosopher tries to see the meaning of the facts which the historian collects, and to discover the necessity at the heart of their contingency. It is important to notice that Hegel brought to the writing of this book an extensive study of the facts whose inward and moving principle he here professes to expound, and thus he is very far from attempting to deduce the philosophy of the state by *a priori* thinking.[34]

One "scientific" approach to the study of states Hegel very explicitly eschews. And that is the prescriptive approach, the aim of which is to construct a theory of the state as it "ought to be," so that statesmen (or youthful "idealists") may set about reconstituting their actual states on the scientist's model. His own object, he says, is the same as that of the astronomer studying the phenomena of the heavens, which is certainly not to teach men how the heavenly bodies "ought to move." "To consider a thing rationally," writes Hegel, "means not to bring reason to bear on the object from the outside and so to tamper with it, but to find that the object is rational on its own account."[35] This is true not only of the purely observational sciences, but also of those founded on experimentation. The experimenter certainly tampers with things in putting his experiment together; but once the experiment has been "made," his task is simply to describe and formulate the rational law implicit in it, without further tampering.

So it is with the study of the man-made state: its rationality has been built into it in the course of history by the generations of men who made it. The state is infinitely more complex than a man-made experiment in a laboratory, but it is, as we noted before, of the same order. Even in the laboratory, the scientist discounts unessential factors and speaks of "other things being equal." Similarly of the object of study of political science, Hegel says: "The state is no ideal work of art; it stands on earth, and so in the sphere of caprice, chance, and error; and bad behavior may disfigure it in many respects. But even the ugliest of men, or a criminal, or an invalid, or a cripple, is still always a living man. The affirmative, life, subsists despite his defects, and it is this affirmative factor [other things being equal] which is our theme here."[36]

According to its "ratio of truth," the state is known first as rationally constituted in itself (Constitutional Law), then as constituted for others (International Law), and finally as adequately linking its domestic and foreign relations in the unity of its role in World History. The state, Hegel repeatedly stresses, is the actuality of concrete freedom. It is free *in itself* and also *for others*. Its internal freedom is so articulated, constitutionally, as to guarantee maximum subjective freedom (diversity in civil society) with maximum objective freedom (unity of purpose in foreign relations). "Sovereignty" is the historical term for the constituted freedom of a politically united people. In its domestic aspect, sovereignty is the effective unity of the citizens, as producers and consumers of the commonwealth, expressed through the legislative processes; and of the wisdom of the "civil" servants, or public-oriented elites, who in the process of administering the law take notice of the difficulties and unanticipated needs that inevitably arise.

But it is in its foreign-relations aspect that the constituted freedom of a politically united people — its sovereignty — is fully manifest. Hegel's words on this aspect of the subject have a tremendous bearing on the question of knowledge as it pertains to political science; for what is at issue here is the reality of statehood as it has been historically defined. The basis of all Right, Hegel says, is "personality"; and hence the imperative of Right is: "Be a person and respect others as persons."[37] States emerge historically to give every man's personality its due, to realize the freedom of personality in its fullness, equally for all, as far as possible. In the more perfect union of a state, the freedom of personality takes on the individuality of the whole. And Hegel says of it:

> Individuality is awareness of one's existence as a unit in sharp distinction from others. It manifests itself on the level of the state as a relation to other states, each of which is autonomous vis-à-vis the others. This autonomy embodies mind's actual awareness of itself as a unit and hence it is the most fundamental freedom which a people possesses as well as its highest dignity . . . . Those who talk of the "wishes" of a "collection" of people to renounce its own political center and autonomy in order to unite with others to form a new whole, have very little knowledge of what a "collection" is or of the feeling of selfhood which a nation possesses in its independence.[38]

The contemporary world has heard so many voices — especially in the academy — cry out against this traditional notion of sovereignty that it has been a relief in recent years to hear the statesmen of the new state of Israel proclaim it at the top of their lungs, often against the combined self-deluding ignorance of what in the Old Testament is termed the gentiles, or "other" nations. The Israeli people have, of course, saved and planned for almost 2,000 years to make a place for themselves in this world — an objective place where, as Free Minds, they can live and govern themselves autonomously. During that interval, they have enjoyed all kinds of freedoms elsewhere, especially in England, France, and the United States; but for the Jews who think of themselves as essentially Jews, wherever they may happen to live in the world, those lesser freedoms — the freedoms of civil society — have never sufficed. The freedom they have sought, and now hope to realize in Palestine, is that sovereign freedom of autonomous statehood that Hegel characterizes as "the most fundamental freedom which a people possesses as well as its highest dignity."

The realization of freedom in autonomous states

that face one another in the world like individualized
personalities in civil society makes up, according to Hegel,
the course of world history. World history "contains" the
histories of individual states, even as the states "contain"
the development of their constituent families and group-
ings of civil society which, in turn, "contain" the lives of
their individual members.

The philosophical science of history, therefore,
presupposes all that has gone before in the exposition of
the sciences of Objective Mind. But here it is the coming to
be and passing away of states in their *relations* with one
another that is the distinguishably new object of scientific
study. The method, however, remains the same; and in his
lectures on the *Philosophy of History*, Hegel once again cites
the practice of astronomers to justify his own scientific
procedure. The astronomer doesn't come to the study of
celestial phenomena with a blank mind. He comes to it with
a mind full of the best ideas of mathematics and mechanics.
Similarly, the serious social scientist doesn't come to the
study of civil society, or the state, with a blank mind. And
just as the concepts of Mind, Freedom, and Will are
presupposed in the scientific study of family life, civil
society, and statehood, so the concepts of statehood and
related concepts (tribe, people, nation) must be presupposed in the scientific study of the so-called facts of history
which cannot of themselves constitute an academic discipline. Against the naive notion of "facts" that can write
themselves up into a science on a *tabula rasa,* Hegel observes:

> That a particular distinction is in fact the characteristic
> principle of a people is the element of our study that
> must be empirically ascertained and historically demon-
> strated. To do this requires, however, that we bring to
> the task not only a disciplined faculty of abstraction but
> also a long familiarity with the Idea. One must have what
> you may call, if you like, *a priori* knowledge, or long
> familiarity with the entire sphere of principles to which

the specific principle in question belongs — just as Kepler (to name only the most celebrated scientist of this sort) must have been acquainted *a priori* with ellipses, cubes, squares and concepts of their interrelationships, before he could discover from the empirical data those immortal laws which are determinations of that sphere of representations. A person ignorant of such elemental concepts and distinctions will fail to understand — let alone discover — such laws no matter how long a time he spends contemplating the sky and the motions of celestial bodies.[39]

In his extended discussion of methods that makes up the introduction to his *Philosophy of History,* Hegel distinguishes Original History, Reflective History, and Philosophical History, showing how the facts or things of the first are to be adequately linked together with the thoughts. or principles of the second in the truth of the third. As Professor J. N. Findlay correctly sums it up:

> The Hegelian Philosophy of History therefore builds on the original histories which constitute the source-material for the past, and also on the more reflective histories which subject this source-material to various critical tests . . . . It only differs from both [in that] its aim is . . . to discover in past States different stages in the developing consciousness of Right, to discover a *line* of development running through all such stages, and to show, further, how events which seem unconnected with this development have none the less contributed to it."[40]

The developing consciousness of Right in history is, of course, the development of freedom. It is in becoming aware of history as the work of Free Mind that the individual mind, first, and then the mind of a people acting together, becomes fully free. The longing for realized freedom is the motive power of human conduct on all levels of the world of Objective Mind, but particularly on that of universal history. "When individuals and nations have once seized upon the abstract idea of freedom itself,"

Hegel says, "it has more than any other thing, boundless power, just because it is the very being of Mind, its very reality."[41]

But universal recognition that Mind is free in its essential being has been slow in coming. Whole continents have known nothing of genuine freedom; and even the Greeks and Romans mistook it for something attached to specially privileged races or to be acquired through privileged education. Only with the spread of the Judeo-Christian religion did the idea take root that freedom is the essential characteristic of manhood. Man, Christianity teaches, is intended inherently for the highest freedom — which is oneness with God. And through that teaching, Christianity has realized in its adherents — first in Europe but eventually elsewhere as well — an "ever-present sense that they are not and cannot be slaves"; so that, "if they are made slaves, if the decision as regards their property rests with an arbitrary will, not with laws or courts of justice, they would find their very substance outraged." This will for freedom, Hegel concludes, "is no longer an *urge* demanding satisfaction; it is very character itself — its being, without urgings, become spiritual consciousness."[42]

In the ancient history of the Far and Near East, the political freedom of states (the united willingness of citizens to die rather than suffer enslavement) was a reality only in the head of state: the single person who exercised such freedom in behalf of his subjects. Thus in the Ancient East, as also in its fossilized modern continuations, only *one* person in each free state was actually free. In the history of the classical world, on the shores of the Mediterranean, political freedom was much more widely experienced; *many* in the free states of Athens, Sparta, and Rome were personally free — though not yet all. In modern history, quite uniquely, freedom has at last become a recognized possibility, and is rapidly on its way to becoming an actuality, for *all.* As Hegel foresaw, all the traditionally enslavable peoples of the world — not only in Black America but in

Black Africa and Yellow Asia as well — are rapidly becoming genuinely free through their newly asserted, manifest willingness to die rather than suffer enslavement.

The Political and Historical Moments of Truth

But it is not when political freedom first becomes possible — as in the backward, newly emerging nations of the world — that the truth of the social, political, and historical experience of man can be known. The awakening and flowering of scientific knowledge is itself deeply rooted in the course of history. It has its proper places and times, its propitious moments of truth, in politics as well as history. We noted earlier that the completed system of philosophical sciences has no privileged beginning. But the same cannot be said of the *impulse* to philosophize. An individual may conceivably begin to pursue true knowledge, in a scientific manner with respect to any conceivable object of knowledge whether mathematical or astronomical, biological or psychological, economic or sociological, etc.; but he can in fact do so only if he happens to have been reared in a society sufficiently advanced politically to assure him the leisure without which a scientific pursuit of knowledge is neither desirable nor possible.

In the opening pages of his *History of Philosophy,* Hegel cites Aristotle's words on the subject, agreeing that the desire to know, as an end in itself, becomes a pressing need only when "almost all the necessities of life and the things that make for comfort and recreation have been secured."[43] The possibility of satisfying such a need, even more than its awakening, presupposes the actuality of a politically advanced society with a considerable history behind it. Doubt, or wonder in the Aristotelian sense, which animates the need to philosophize, is not excited into being simply by man's awareness of his natural environment. The hungry man does not "wonder" about the food he needs to eat, any more than he wonders about the "nature" of the beast who attacks him when he is out hunting or about the nature of the pleasure he gets in gratifying his hunger or his sexual appetite. Before the wonder that leads to science can be awakened, the animal cravings must have disappeared, and so must the immediate fears; and in their place, as Hegel expresses it, "a strength, elevation, and moral fortitude of mind must have appeared, passions must be subdued and consciousness advanced to the point that its thinking is free and not self-seeking."[44] It is the point in the cycle of the sciences of Subjective Mind where, as a consequence of self-analysis, Mind is at last free to overcome its subjectivity.

Self-analysis of that sort is not possible among primitive peoples. The beginnings of true science are thus reserved for advanced societies; and even in advanced societies, one particular phase of historical development is much more suitable for such beginnings than any other. Hegel emphasizes that, for a genuine awakening of scientific curiosity,

> thought must be for itself, must come into existence in its freedom, liberate itself from nature and come out of its immersion in sense-perception; it must, as free, enter within itself and thus arrive at the consciousness of freedom .... If we say that the consciousness of freedom is connected with the development of philosophy, this principle must be a fundamental one in the people among whom philosophy begins .... Connected with this on the practical side, is the fact that actual freedom develops political freedom, [so that, objectively,] philosophy appears in history only where and insofar as free institutions are formed.[45]

In other words, the mind that can freely philosophize is the same Free Mind which, after experiencing the moral frustration of attempting to press claims of abstract personal right, realizes itself in the actualities of family-life, civil society, statehood, and the universal history of states. Free men constitute states, states make history; and it is in the course of the universal history of states — from the found-

ing of the first historical states in the great river-valley
civilizations of the ancient Far and Near East down through
the ages of ancient Greece and Rome and of the medieval
and modern peoples — that Mind frees itself from temporal
things to become Absolute in Art, Religion and Philosophy. In Hegel's words:

> It may be said that Philosophy first commences when a
> race [broadest extension of family-life] has largely left its
> concrete mode of existence [constituted statehood],
> when separation and change of class have begun [expan-
> sion of civil society], and the community is approaching
> its decline . . . . This holds good throughout all the
> history of philosophy . . . . Thus in Athens, with the ruin
> of the Athenian people, the period was reached when
> philosophy appeared . . . . In Rome, philosophy first
> developed in the decline of the Republic. [And] it was
> with the decline of the Empire that the height and indeed
> the zenith of ancient philosophy was attained in the
> systems of the neo-Platonists at Alexandria.[46]

The questioning of experience that results in the
flowering of science and philosophy is the same questioning that consumes the social order by undermining its
authority. For that reason it can be said that, while in the
experience of any one person, wonder may rise to the level
of systematic doubt at any point around the great circle of
knowledge, historically it has awakened first within the
range of the social, political, and historical consciousness
of man. Excited by doubt, Mind invariably brings its quest
for truth to focus, first of all, on its own social environment: which is to say, on the "institutions and forms of
government of the people among whom it makes its appearance; their morality, their social life and capabilities,
customs and enjoyments; their attempts and achievements
in art and science; their religious experience; their wars
and foreign relations; and lastly, the origin and progress of
the states arising to displace them."[47]

When animated by doubt, when pursued questioningly, mind "subverts" what it studies. That was the charge raised against Socrates by the Athenian democracy; and it was a valid charge. But, as Hegel represents it, in condemning Socrates the Athenians were really condemning themselves. For Socrates was, in fact, the Athenian Mind itself committed to self-criticism. In every age of intense philosophical study, the studying mind and the historical actuality which it studies mirror one another, and are indeed one. On this theme Hegel says in the *History of Philosophy:* "Mind takes refuge in the clear space of thought to create for itself a kingdom of thought in opposition to the world of actuality, and Philosophy is the reconciliation following upon the destruction of that real world — a destruction which thought has begun."[48]

Hegel's philosophical sciences of society, politics, and history are thus mirrors of a dissolving world. Thought consumes its own objectivization of itself in space and time as objectively inadequate. True philosophy, like true art and true religion, transcends the realities of politics and history. It is utterly wrong, therefore, to try to make a secular optimist out of Hegel. What optimism is to be found in his philosophic system pertains to a sphere beyond history, and therefore beyond the associational life of family, civil society, and statehood that makes up the pattern of history.

"Passions, private aims, and the satisfaction of selfish desires are the most effective springs of action in history," writes Hegel, "because they respect none of the limitations which Right and Morality would impose, and because they exert a more direct influence over men than the artificial and tedious discipline that tends toward order and self-restraint, law and morality." Yet, when we read the record of history and note the evil and ruin that such passions, aims, and desires have wrought, when we contemplate the "miseries that have overwhelmed the noblest nations and polities, and the finest examples of private virtue," we experience, Hegel writes, "mental torture, allowing no defense or escape but the consideration that what has happened could not be otherwise; that it is a fatality which no intervention could alter." It is out of a history that "excites emotions of the profoundest and most hopeless sadness" that we pass into the sphere of Absolute Mind.[49] The transition is the flight of Minerva's owl — which is possible only after the long day's task is done. Philosophy's backward glance on the wreckage of political history is a tragic theodicy.

One must stress the pessimism of the Hegelian doctrine of Objective Mind to avoid the popular error that would make of him an idolater of statehood and the historical process. The state is for Hegel, as for St. Augustine and the Founding Fathers of the United States, a necessary evil. Men initially build up the edifice of human society, he says, to gratify their passions; but they end up "fortifying a position of Right and Order against themselves."[50] The passionate aims of individuals are checked and balanced in the rationality of states; and the self-centered interests of states are checked and balanced in the hard trials of universal history. That history is by no means a theater of happiness. On the contrary, its periods of happiness are no more than blank pages, signifying nothing.

To make a worldly optimist out of Hegel, one must either decapitate him, denying his doctrine of art, religion, and God-centered philosophy, as Croce and the fascist humanists generally have done; or turn his entire doctrine upside down, as Marx and the materialist humanists have done. Right side up and whole, Hegel must rank with St. Augustine among the profoundest worldly pessimists of Christendom, even as he must rank with Aristotle — *il maestro di color che sanno* – among the greatest of systematic philosophers who have concerned themselves with the sciences of society, politics, and history.

NOTES

1. *The Logic of Hegel* (Part I of *Enzyklopädie*), trans., William Wallace (Oxford, 1892) pp. 28-29 (§ 18). This work is hereafter cited as *HL*; translations adapted slightly in accordance with German text (Henning, 1840, 1955).

2. *Hegel's Science of Logic*, trans. W. H. Johnston and L. G. Struthers (London, 1951), Vol. II, p. 227.

3. *Hegel's Philosophy of Mind* (Part III of *Enzyklopädie*), trans. W. Wallace and A. V. Miller (Oxford, 1971), p. 180 (§440). This work is hereafter cited as *PhM*; translations adapted slightly in accordance with German text (Boumann, I958).

4. *The Phoenomenology of Mind*, trans, J. B. Baillie (London, 1931), p. 90; adapted slightly (Hoffmeister, 1949).

5. *HL*, p. 59 (§ 25).

6. *HL, ibid.*

7. *HL*, p. 28 (§ 17).

8. *HL*, pp. 24-25 (§ 14, 15).

9. *HL, ibid.*

10. *The Basic Works of Aristotle*, ed. Richard McKeon (New York, 1941), p. 41 (adapted in accordance with Bekker, *De Interpretatione*, 16ᵇ 19-25).

11. *Hegel's Lectures on the History of Philosophy*, trans. E. S. Haldane and Frances H. Simson (London, 1955), Vol. II, p. 223. This work is hereafter cited as *HPh*; translations adapted slightly in accordance with German text (Michelet, 1840).

12. *PhM*, p. 3 (§ 378).

13. *Hegel's Philosophy of Right*, trans. T. M. Knox (Oxford, 1956), p. 106 (§ 146). This work is hereafter cited as *PhR*; translations adapted slightly in accordance with German text (Gans 1833, 1932), making use also of the translation by S. W. Dyde (London, 1896).

14. *PhR*, p. 4 (Preface).

15. *Aristotle's Politics*, trans. H. Rackbam (Camb., Mass. and London, 1950), p. 11 (1253ª).

16. *Ibid.*

17. *PhR*, pp. 264-5 (note to § 173).

18. *PhR*, pp. 117-118 (§ 175).

19. *PhR*, pp. 266-7 (note to § 182).

20. *PhR*, p. 266 (note to § 182).

21. *PhR*, p. 267 (note to § 182).

22. *PhR*, pp. 126-7 (§ 189).

23. *PhR*, p. 268 (note to § 189).

24. *PhR*, p. 150 (§ 244).

25. *Ibid.*, § 245.

26. *PhR*, pp. 151-2 (§ 246, 248).

27. *PhR*, p. 278 (note to § 248).

28. *Aristotle's Politics*, op. cit., p. 29 (1255b20).

29. Herbert Croly, *The Promise of American Life* (Indianapolis, 1965), p. 395.

30. *PhR*, pp. 153, 278 (§ 253 and note to § 255).

31. *PhR*, p. 154 (§ 255) and p. 155 (§ 256).

32. *PhM*, p. 130 (§ 408).

33. *PhM*, p. 265 (§ 539).

34. *PhR*, p. 306.

35. *PhR*, p. 35 (§ 31).

36. *PhR*, p. 279 (note to § 258).

37. *PhR* p. 37 (§ 36).

38. *PhR*, p. 208 (§ 322).

39. Hegel's *Philosophy of History*, trans. J, Sibree (New York, 1956), p. 64. Translation adapted slightly in accordance with German text (Lasson, 1930).

40. J. N. Findlay, *Hegel: A Re-examination* (New York, 1962), p. 334.

41. *PhM*, p. 239 (§ 482).

42. *PhM*, p. 240 (§ 482).

43. *HPh*, Vol. I, p. 51.

44. *HPh, ibid.*

45. *HPh*, Vol. I, pp. 94-5.

46. *HPh*, Vol. I, pp. 52-3.

47. *HPh*, Vol. I, p. 53.

48. *HPh*, Vol. I, p. 52.

49. Hegel's *Philosophy of History*, op. cit., pp. 20-21.

50. *Ibid.*, p. 27.